THE
IMPOSED
COVENANT

By Dwayne Norman

Empyrion Publishing
Winter Garden FL
EmpyrionPublishing.com

The Imposed Covenant

Copyright © 2017 by Dwayne Norman

ISBN: 978-0-9981013-6-1

Empyrion Publishing
PO Box 784327
Winter Garden FL 34778
info@EmpyrionPublishing.com

Unless otherwise noted, all Scripture quotations are
from the New King James Version of the Bible.

Printed in the United States of America

Table of Contents

CHAPTER
1

THE NIGHT THE DEVIL GOT IN BED WITH ME

It was a snowy winter night in Lexington, Kentucky about 23 years ago and I had just gone to bed at 1 o'clock in the morning. I lived in a one-story home and my bedroom was in the back of the house down the hallway from the front door. As soon as I closed my eyes I heard what sounded like someone trying very loudly to open my front door. It seemed that whoever was doing this was not trying to be quiet about it.

Normally, I would have assumed it was the wind blowing against my door, but the sound was so loud I thought maybe someone was trying to break into my house, so I got up to check. I did not want to open the door in case someone was outside so I looked through the window by the front door. That particular night we had a good deal of snow on the ground and it was in pristine condition outside of my door. I figured if someone was trying to break in;

there would be foot prints in the snow. To my surprise there were none.

Walking back to my bedroom I was puzzled. Why did I hear such a loud noise at my front door, as if someone was attempting to break off my door knob? I was glad that I did not see any footprints but yet I was still bothered by the whole ordeal. I saw no evidence of foul play, yet I was very alarmed at the loud noise I heard. I went ahead and got in bed and pulled the covers over me. While lying on my back, my eyes closed, and my hands wresting on my stomach, my thought was to go to sleep and get a good night's rest, but that didn't happen right at first; things around me quickly changed.

I immediately felt the bed go down next to my left foot, as if somebody was in bed with me! My left foot slid over into the indention made in the bed. I thought it had to be a person with his foot or knee pressing down on my bed, but I really did not want to look. As much as I did not want to open my eyes, I knew that I could not just lay there and hope that the person would leave. So, I quickly decided that I would jump up in the bed as fast as I could and start swinging at whoever was there.

I jumped up, opened my eyes with my fists in front of me and to my complete surprise there was no one in the room. Suddenly, my room filled with evil, the presence of the devil, probably one of his demons. I knew immediately this was not a natural fight but a spiritual one. I spoke to the devil and said, "I know you're the one who pushed my bed down to scare me, and I bind you in Jesus' Name! I command you to get out of my room and my house! I plead the Blood of Jesus against you!!"

As soon as I began to plead the Blood, the devil left immediately! It was as if a spiritual vacuum cleaner sucked his evil presence out of the room! I then fell backwards onto my bed and slept soundly until 9 o'clock in the morning. I did not have a bad dream or wake up one time. I believe that God put me to sleep that night. I knew how powerful the Blood of Jesus was but this experience gave me a much greater reality of that! Jesus' precious Blood is covenant Blood! As Christians, we are in a new and eternal Blood covenant with God! The reason we are in this new covenant is because we are in Christ and washed white as snow through His perfect and holy Blood!

Whatever the devil is bringing against you right now, you need to spiritually stand up and resist it with all your faith in God! Command the devil to take his hands off you, your body, your marriage, your finances and your children in Jesus' Name!! Plead the Blood of Jesus against him and expect him to leave! Remember, the Bible says that if we submit to God and resist the devil, he will flee from us (James 4:7)! Also, the Lord told you and me to cast the devil out in Jesus' Name (Mark 16:17)! So, if you feel like the devil is trying to get a foothold in any area of your life, cast him out in the Name of Jesus! Mark 16:17 did not say to ask God to cast the devil out, but Jesus told you and me to cast him out. If you don't want to be a part of the devil's program to steal, kill and destroy then command him to leave immediately, and then declare that Jesus is Lord in and over every area of your life!

CHAPTER
2

WHAT IS A BLOOD COVENANT?

In the Bible, the Lord makes a difference between the old covenant and the new covenant. Let's see what He said about that in Hebrews 8:6-13.

"**But now He has obtained a more excellent ministry, inasmuch as He is also Mediator of a better covenant, which was established on better promises.**

For if that first covenant had been faultless, then no place would have been sought for a second.

Because finding fault with them, He says: 'Behold, the days are coming, says the Lord, when I will make a new covenant with the house of Israel and with the house of Judah-

not according to the covenant that I made with their fathers in the day when I took them by the hand to lead them out of the land of Egypt; because they did not continue in My covenant, and I disregarded them, says the Lord.

For this is the covenant that I will make with the house of Israel after those days, says the Lord: I will put My laws in their mind and write them on their hearts; and I will be their God, and they shall be My people.

None of them shall teach his neighbor, and none his brother, saying, 'Know the Lord,' for all shall know Me, from the least of them to the greatest of them.

For I will be merciful to their unrighteousness, and their sins and their lawless deeds I will remember no more."

In that He says, "A new covenant." He has made the first obsolete. Now what is becoming obsolete and growing old is ready to vanish away."

This book is not just about defining a blood covenant, but it is about the meaning of an imposed covenant. So, the question we are going to answer is, "What is an imposed covenant"? Also, we are going to see how that relates to being a new creation in Christ. When you become a new person in Christ Jesus (according to Romans 10:9) you enter into Covenant with God. You are now in Christ and He is in you; which is the very definition and essence of this new and eternal Blood covenant. I expect your faith to increase and for you to receive a greater revelation of the grace of God through your understanding of this awesome covenant. If you have not really grasped the meaning of what it means to be in Christ and Christ Jesus in you, this teaching from God's Word (if you will receive it) will greatly solidify and strengthen your understanding.

So, please do not skip over the Scripture verses in an effort to finish this book quickly, but read, ponder and meditate (spiritually eat and digest) every verse in this book. I pray in Jesus' Name that the Lord will teach you and show you how to apply in every area of your life what you will learn in the pages ahead. We are not studying about the Blood covenant for just head knowledge so we can pass a Bible school test, but we want to know how to experience (in full manifestation) all the benefits and blessings of this covenant, and how to walk and live in its fullness! You will soon realize that walking and living in covenant fullness is synonymous with walking and living in Christ (Colossians 2:6-10).

The Bible, of course, is made up of the old and new covenants separated by Calvary. Before the Lord Jesus died and arose from the dead man could not be born again. No one could receive eternal life and be made brand new in his spirit. No one could declare, "I am a son or daughter of God in Christ". People could experience a right standing with God even though their conscience was not cleansed of sin or the nature of sin and death (what the Apostle Paul referred to as the old man, Hebrews 9:14; Romans 6:6). They could become friends of God, and that is very wonderful, but not sons of God; not heirs of God and joint heirs with Jesus (I John 3:2; Romans 8:17).

In this new Blood covenant, we are not only friends of God but we are also His sons and daughters! It is time to learn what it means to be a son of God! Romans 8:19 talks about how all of creation eagerly waits for the revealing and manifestation of the sons of God! In Galatians 1:15-16, Paul said that God called him through His grace to reveal His Son in him. I think it would be good to start prophesying and declaring that God is revealing Jesus in your life and through you everywhere you go, and He is making manifest to those around you the reality that you are a son of God in covenant with Him!! God wants to demonstrate His glory through us this way in drawing the lost to Jesus (Isaiah 60:1-5)!

There are so many blessings the Lord wants us to enjoy, but the most important thing is that we really know and experience Jesus as our first love (Revelation 2:4, 5). From that place of experiencing Jesus as our first love we should be spiritually propelled to go forth with great joy and excitement in fulfilling our mission to win the lost to Jesus and make disciples of all the nations! Remember, serving the Lord is very necessary and important, but don't let your time spent serving God cause you to neglect your time spent getting to know Him; not just as your Lord and Savior but in deeper and more intimate fellowship. Understanding your relationship with God through the Blood covenant will serve as a catalyst in experiencing greater intimacy with Him.

This will make better sense to you when you understand that God's Blood covenant is a result of our union with Christ, and that union is based on relationship. Listen to what Psalm 25:14 says in the Amplified Bible.

"The secret [of the wise counsel] of the LORD is for those who fear Him, and He will let them know His covenant and reveal to them [through His word] its [deep, inner] meaning."

It seems to me that God is making a connection between knowing the secret (wise counsel) of the Lord and our understanding of His covenant. The greater revelation I receive of my union with Christ in Blood covenant, the more the Lord will reveal His secret things to me. Doesn't that sound exciting? I want to know the Father God, the Lord Jesus and the Holy Spirit in the deepest, richest way possible, don't you? Therefore, to experience this kind of fellowship, I need my comprehension and insight into this covenant greatly increased.

In the first chapter I shared the story of how great power is manifested when by faith you plead and speak the Blood of Jesus. Please remember that the precious Blood of Jesus and the right to plead His Blood is a covenant benefit. It is one of our covenant rights. Learning about our covenant relationship with the Lord is learning about all of our rights and privileges in Christ. Throughout this book I want you to get the revelation that being in covenant with God means being in Christ and Christ in you. Being in Christ is a covenant and relationship term. If you have not read our book "In Christ- True Purpose, True Peace, True Fulfillment" I hope you will visit our website for that. You can find it at www.dwaynenormanministries.org. We also have 70 audio messages (about 13 minutes each) on youtube.com under "Dwayne Norman Your Identity in Christ".

According to the Strong's Concordance, the Hebrew definition of a covenant is a cutting and a compact made by passing between pieces of flesh. According to W. E. Vine expository dictionary, a covenant is a coming together between two parties or more, each binding himself to fulfill certain obligations. Since the very definition of a covenant has to do with a cutting or animal sacrifice, the shedding of blood is always involved. If you study the different covenants made by people throughout the centuries, you will find many similarities. One such similarity is they were binding unto death. A covenant made between two parties was a very serious obligation and the most binding of relationships.

When you understand how binding and serious this agreement was between two human beings then you will begin to recognize even more so how unbreakable the Blood covenant is between God and Jesus.

"And this I say, that the law, which was four hundred and thirty years later, cannot annul the covenant that was confirmed before by God <u>in Christ</u>, that it should make the promise of no effect." (Galatians 3:17)

Now, what I just said may have raised a question in your mind. You are probably wondering why the Bible says this covenant was made between God and Jesus. In your mind, you may have thought that this covenant was between God and Believers, and if that was your understanding, you would be very correct; but the way God chose to bring us into this Blood covenant was through Jesus; through His Son representing us. Because of the nature of a blood covenant, by making it with Jesus, our representative, He was making it with us.

Remember, as a Christian, you are <u>in Christ</u>. Let me repeat that again. God made this new covenant with Jesus so that He could make it with you. Why did He do that? That was the only way He could get you involved in it. If He made it only between you and Himself then it could be broken; not on God's side but on yours. By making this covenant with Jesus, it cannot fail! Now, we can fail to operate in it and enjoy the benefits of it, but we cannot destroy God's covenant. Here are a few Scriptures on how our Heavenly Father was working <u>in Christ</u> for you and me before the foundation of the world.

"**All who dwell on the earth will worship him, whose names have not been written in the Book of Life of the Lamb <u>slain from the foundation of the world.</u>**" (Revelation 13:8)

"**He indeed was foreordained before the foundation of the world, but was manifest in these last times for you.**" (I Peter 1:20)

"**Just as He chose us <u>in Him</u> <u>before the foundation of the</u> <u>world</u>, that we should be holy and without blame before Him in love.**" (Ephesians 1:4, emphasis added throughout chapter)

"**That is, that God was <u>in Christ</u> <u>reconciling the world to</u> <u>Himself</u>, not imputing their trespasses to them, and has committed to us the word of reconciliation.**" (II Corinthians 5:19)

"**And be kind to one another, tenderhearted, forgiving one another, even as God <u>in Christ</u> <u>forgave you</u>.** (Ephesians 4:32)

"**That the Gentiles should be fellow heirs, of the same body, and <u>partakers of His promise in Christ</u> through the gospel.**" (Ephesians 3:6)

"According to the <u>eternal purpose which He accomplished</u> in Christ Jesus our Lord." (Ephesians 3:11)

God knew ahead of time what Adam and Eve would do and how He would fix it. He planned before man was created and before the foundation of the world to have a family; sons and daughters born of His Spirit who would worship, fellowship with and serve Him from their own free wills with all of their hearts. He knew that the way to accomplish this would involve a Blood covenant with His people. He also knew that a covenant between Him and man alone could be broken on man's side; so He came up with an ingenious idea. He made this covenant between Himself and the Lord Jesus. Remember, God cannot lie, fail or change. Therefore, this Blood covenant was made between God the Father and God the Son. It is an eternal covenant that will never fail!

At the same time that God came up with this great idea, He also came up with a Divine plan on how to legally place you and me in this unfailing covenant. He chose Jesus as the Key to accomplish this awesome plan. Jesus came to this earth and totally identified Himself with man (male and female) so man could be totally identified with Him through all that He suffered and finished in His death and resurrection. Through Jesus fully representing us, paying our penalty for sin, He satisfied God's laws of justice, so we could be made new creations in Christ. When we were place in Christ and Christ in us, we were automatically translated into God's Kingdom and into Blood covenant with Him!

So, if we will find out how to operate in God's Blood covenant it will always work for us! His Covenant and the Word of His covenant cannot fail! I hope this helps you to better understand why you must be <u>in Christ</u> (born again) to participate in this Blood covenant.

Let me say this before I go any further in this book. I know that you are probably a Christian, but if you are not 100% sure you are in Christ, you can be sure right now. Just say this pray to God and believe it in your heart and you will be saved. Say this with me, "Lord Jesus, I believe that you died, shed your Blood and arose from the dead for me. Please come into my heart and life and make me a brand new person, and I now confess that you are my Lord and Savior. Thank you, Father, for saving me in Jesus' Name!" If you just prayed that and meant it from your heart, you are now a Christian and in covenant with God.

If you have studied a lot about blood covenants, I want to remind you in the pages ahead about some different aspects of a blood covenant you may not have thought about. If you haven't studied much about blood covenants then this will be fresh and new to you. This teaching is by no means an exhaustive study on blood covenants. It is what I believe the Lord wants me to share with you to help you experience greater victory in your walk with the Lord.

So, let's look more into what a blood covenant was all about. For instance, when two tribes or groups of people began the process of entering into a covenant, they would first get a representative. If you have spent much time learning about your redemption in Christ, you will probably hear some terms and phrases that you did not realize are actually covenant terms and phrases. I pray that you will start seeing the connection.

The first thing the two parties would do is to get a representative man to stand in for them. This man represented each party or group of people in the covenant. Does that sound familiar? Whatever this representative man said and did was considered the same as if the party he represented had said the same words and performed the same actions. As we go along, I am going to remind you of some Scriptures that you have probably read before, but I want to show how they relate to our covenant with God. I Corinthians 15:21 says, **"For as in Adam all die, even so in Christ all shall be made alive."** When I teach on the Mystery of Christ (see our book "The Mystery" on our website) I bring out the point that Adam and Jesus were the two most important men in the Bible. They were not the most important men because they worked the most miracles or had the biggest ministries. They were the most important men because they were the only two men in history to represent the entire human race.

If you think about it, the first covenant ever made with the human race was probably between Adam and God. Adam represented every person who would ever be born. You may be thinking how do we know that? The verse we just read in Corinthians said that all people died in Adam when he died. If Adam did not represent everyone then everyone would not have died in him. Romans 5:12 says that through one man (Adam), death spread to all men. But, the good news (Gospel) is that Jesus represented all men so when He was made alive from spiritual death to spiritual life so were we. Our Lord obtained eternal life for all of humanity. We were made alive in Him! In Christ Jesus we conquered the devil; we were resurrected and seated at the right hand of God in His throne room (Ephesians 2:4-6)!! This is what Jesus finished for us, but it will not automatically come to pass in our lives, we must receive it by faith.

All that I have been teaching about the mystery of Christ (the mystery Paul identified in Ephesians chapter 3 and Colossians 1:26, 27) is really covenant terminology. All that our Lord finished for us and blessed us with through His entire substitutionary sacrifice was so that we could enter into this Blood covenant made between the Father and the Son. Isn't it wonderful and glorious to be in Christ and in Blood covenant with Almighty God?

After each party got a representative, they would then get an animal, normally a heifer, they would lay it on the ground and cut it down the middle; of course, blood would spread everywhere. Both representatives would then walk back and forth in the blood between the two pieces sometimes making a figure 8 which symbolized infinity. By their actions they were declaring that this covenant is binding unto death for the rest of their lives and could extend to their children. Remember the covenant made between David and Johnathan? After Johnathan had died David found his son Mephibosheth so he could bless him because of the covenant he had made with his father.

Now, don't forget what the two representatives were there for. As they walked through this blood it was the same as if all the parties involved were walking through all the blood. They were walking through the blood for the people they represented. Let me ask you this? Did Jesus shed His Blood for Himself? No, He represented us. We are the ones who needed our sins washed away but we could not do it with our blood; so He bled for us, in our place. The precious Blood that covered Jesus (since He was our representative) has now covered us and washed us white as snow (Hebrews 9:22).

While the two representatives walked through the blood they began to pronounce the blessings and curses which would accompany the covenant (Deuteronomy chapter 28 talks about that). They let each other know that all that I have is yours, all my wealth, riches and protection. They also committed to one another to always be there if either one needed help. Doesn't that sound like what our covenant partner said to us? **The Lord is my Shepherd; I shall not want** (Psalm 23). **My God will supply all my need according to His riches in glory by Christ Jesus** (Philippians 4:19). **I dwell in the secret place of the most High** (Psalm 91), and so many other great Scriptures. If you think about it, the Scriptures in the Bible are the Word of this Blood covenant. I believe after you read this book, you will become much more conscience and aware of your covenant God every time you read the Bible.

When the two representatives were announcing what the curses would be, they would remind each other of the consequences of breaking this agreement. Those consequences could include the same fate that their animal sacrifice experienced; thus emphasizing, that this covenant is binding unto death. That kind of commitment to stay loyal and true to someone is hard to find in the world today. In our society people make agreements, sign contracts and do not think twice about breaking them! They do not have a clue what faithfulness and integrity are all about. When our Heavenly Father said that He cannot lie, He was revealing a quality of His nature but also describing His commitment to faithfully honor the Blood covenant He made with us in Christ. Some of the first Scriptures that I memorized when I was a teenager described God's integrity. They were verses which declared that God cannot lie (Numbers 23:19; Hebrews 6:18 and Titus 1:2). I did not realize that those verses were covenant terms.

One such Scripture was spoken by the Lord in John 10:35, **"If He called them gods, to whom the word of God came (and the Scripture cannot be broken)."** When Jesus said the Scripture cannot be broken, He was using a covenant phrase. He was reminding them that God's Blood covenant cannot be broken.

Many times, after walking through the blood, the two representatives would make a cut around their wrist and bring them together thereby mingling their blood; showing they had become one with each other. Again remember, all that these two men were doing was for the benefit of the parties they represented. Every time you read about the sufferings of Jesus and all that He did at Calvary, you are actually reading about yourself and all that God did in you and for you through Jesus. The Lord Jesus did not do anything for Himself when He came here.

He <u>totally</u> identified with us so that we could be <u>totally</u> identified with Him in all that He finished for us!

In some areas of the world, after these representatives mingled their blood through the joining of their wrists they would rub gun powder or something else into the wound to cause it to scar up. They used this as a symbol to identify that they were in a blood covenant with someone. God told Abraham in Genesis 17:10, 11:

"This is My covenant which you shall keep, between Me and you and your descendants after you: Every male child among you shall be circumcised;
And you shall be circumcised in the flesh of your foreskins, and it shall be a sign of the covenant between Me and you."

Physical circumcision was a sign that you were in covenant with God in the Old Testament. In the New Testament or new covenant, we still have circumcision, but it is a spiritual circumcision and is called the circumcision of Christ. All born again men and women have received it. Colossians 2:11 says:

"In Him you were also circumcised with the circumcision made without hands, by putting off the body of the sins of the flesh, by the circumcision of Christ."

To circumcise means to cut around or to cut away the foreskin. In the old covenant the male children were physically circumcised, but in the new covenant we have been spiritually circumcised. Let me explain. When you confessed Jesus as your Lord and Savior the Holy Spirit came into your human spirit and cut away and removed that old nature of sin and death (the old man) and gave you a new nature; the nature of God - eternal life - righteousness and love. I am talking about a spiritual circumcision. Through Jesus' death and resurrection, He killed and destroyed the old you and made you into a new you (Romans chapter 6). When you received the circumcision of Christ is when you became a new creation in Him (II Corinthians 5:17). The circumcision of Christ is a sign of this new Blood covenant. You cannot see it with your natural eyes, but God can. He knows those who belong to Him; yes, those who are in His family; His sons and daughters.

I want us to go back to the reason these two covenant partners left a scar on their wrist. If one of the partners found himself in a precarious situation where his life was being threatened by dangerous people, he could just hold up his wrist and show them his scar. If they knew anything about a blood covenant they would think twice before attacking him. They may have assumed they could defeat and kill him, but when they saw that scar on his wrist they knew that he had a covenant partner and they did not know how powerful his partner was. If they had any sense they would leave this man alone or his covenant partner would hunt them down and inflict the same harm on them they were about to unleash on him. That covenant scar would have saved his life.

When the devil comes to attack you with his fear, doubt, sickness, financial lack and depression just hold up your arm (spiritually speaking) and let him see that covenant scar. He knows you are in Blood covenant with God and have been sealed with the Holy Spirit and the circumcision of Christ. A good example of this is in Acts 19:13-16.

"Then some of the itinerant Jewish exorcists took it upon themselves to call the name of the Lord Jesus over those who had evil spirits, saying, "We exorcise you by the Jesus whom Paul preaches."
Also there were seven sons of Sceva, a Jewish chief priest, who did so.
And the evil spirit answered and said, "Jesus I know, and Paul I know; but who are you?"
Then the man in whom the evil spirit was leaped on them, over powered them, and prevailed against them, so that they fled out of that house naked and wounded."

The demon spirit knew that Jesus and Paul were in a covenant with God but these Jewish exorcists were not. This spirit knew that these Jewish exorcists did not have a covenant partner; there was no one to stand with them and fight for them. The devil knows who I am, and I hope that he knows who you are. If you are in Christ then he does. He also knows that if he messes with you he is messing with Almighty God, but he's hoping that you do not know that. He's hoping that you have not learned who you are in Christ. He's hoping that you don't know how to operate in faith and exercise your Blood covenant rights.

Once the two representatives finished mingling their blood together from their wrist they would then partake of a covenant meal, which could be made up of bread and wine. I hope that you see the Biblical inference here to Communion or the Lord's Supper. I am going to talk more about this in a later chapter, but many times they would feed each other this meal (like a husband and wife do at their wedding reception) and say to each other, "As you eat this food you are ingesting me and we are becoming one." Can you see from this the revelation of being in Christ and Christ in you?

Then sometimes the two representatives would exchange their outer robes symbolizing taking on the other person's identity. Haven't we been identified with Christ? When Jesus suffered for us and went to the cross He identified Himself with us so we could be identified with Him. That is why I John 4:17 says that as Jesus is so are we in this world. Once again, covenant terminology. We are identified with Him.

We are not Jesus, but we are His body and we are one spirit with Him. We are bone of His bone and flesh of His flesh (Ephesians 5:30). Remember, we did not have any of this until we accepted God's covenant invitation or His imposed covenant. Also, our Father God has given us His garments, hasn't He? The garment of praise for the spirit of heaviness, the robe of righteousness and His whole armor (Ephesians chapter 6). Praise the Lord!

One last thing I want to share with you about a blood covenant is the exchange of names. God said to Abram in Genesis 17:5, **"No longer shall your name be called Abram, but your name shall be Abraham; for I have made you a father of many nations."** One of the names of God is Yahweh (YHWH) and He took the Hebrew letter for "H" and placed it in Abram's name and it became Abraham. In this new covenant, the Lord Jesus also gave us His Name, didn't He? We have been authorized to use the Name of Jesus when speaking the command of faith and praying the prayer of faith (John 14:12-14; 16:23-24)! Having Jesus' Name is one of our great covenant benefits. Please let me end this chapter by reminding you of what the Lord said in Revelation 3:12.

"He who overcomes, I will make him a pillar in the temple of My God, and he shall go out no more. <u>I will write on him</u> the name of My God <u>and the name of the city of My God</u>, the New Jerusalem,

**which comes down out of heaven from My God, and
<u>I will write on him My new name</u>.**" (Emphasis added
throughout chapter)

CHAPTER
3

THE IMPOSITION

I want to share with you that great story from Genesis 15:5-18 where God made a covenant with Abraham.

"Then He brought him outside and said, 'Look now toward heaven, and count the stars if you are able to number them.' And He said to him, 'So shall your descendants be.'

And he believed in the Lord, and He accounted it to him for righteousness.

Then He said to him, 'I am the Lord, who brought you out of Ur of the Chaldeans, to give you this land to inherit it.'

So He said to him, 'Bring Me a three-year-old heifer, a three-year-old female goat, a three-year-old ram, a turtledove, and a young pigeon.'

Then he brought all these to Him and cut them in two, down the middle, and placed each piece opposite her other; but he did not cut the birds in two.

And when the <u>vultures came down</u> on the carcasses, <u>Abram drove them away</u>.

Now when the sun was going down, a deep sleep fell upon Abram; and behold, horror and great darkness fell upon him.

Then He said to Abram: 'Know certainly that your descendants will be strangers in a land that is not theirs, and will serve them, and they will afflict them four hundred years.

And also the nation whom they serve I will judge; afterward they shall come out with great possessions.

Now as for you, you shall go to your fathers in peace; you shall be buried at a good old age.

But in the fourth generation they shall return here, for the iniquity of the Amorites is not yet complete.'

And it came to pass, when the sun went down and it was dark, that behold, there appeared <u>a smoking oven and a</u> <u>burning torch that passed between those pieces</u>.

On the same day <u>the Lord made a covenant</u> with Abram, saying: 'To your descendants I have given this land...'" (Emphasis added throughout chapter)

There are a number of good books on the market that will give you a detailed understanding about blood covenants, and I am very glad they are available. Yet, in this book, I believe the Lord wants me to bring out an aspect about His covenant that will give you a deeper understanding of its nature. The aspect I want to make you aware of is that this Blood covenant is an **imposed** covenant. I don't know if you have ever thought about that before but when you begin to understand the meaning of an imposed covenant then you will begin to see that it is actually a covenant of grace. By the way, I did briefly touch on this subject in the ninth chapter of my book "The Prosperous Seed", where I am explaining the relationship between grace and sowing and reaping.

In the dictionary, the word "imposition" refers to the action or process of imposing something. Now, when I start talking about an imposition where our Father God is concerned, I want you to also think about the meaning of God's grace in your life. Let me give you an example of an imposition. If I told my wife (Leia) that I wanted her to go to the Mall with me today; that would be an imposition to her, wouldn't it? I would be trying to impose something on her, but now listen, I still would not be overriding her will or forcing her to go to the Mall. I would be strongly encouraging her to go and even telling her that if she would go with me she would be very glad, but still she would have the freedom to choose what she wanted to do wouldn't she? She could say "no" if she wanted to and not yield or submit to my imposition.

No matter how strongly I encouraged her to go with me she could still reject my invitation couldn't she? Think about the same thing in your walk with the Lord. God by His grace demonstrated through the sufferings of Jesus how He obtained for all humanity: eternal life, healing, prosperity, freedom, peace and all the blessings of Heaven. He did all that for humanity but He will not force any of those blessings on us. No matter how wonderful and great His blessings are you must (from your own free will) accept and receive them by faith in God. That is what the grace of God is all about. If you will not choose to release your faith and experience His grace then that is your loss; so don't blame God, your spouse, your pastor, your senator or the president, because they did not force you to turn down God's invitation.

This is what God did when He made a covenant with Abraham in Genesis chapter 15. He imposed it upon him. Look with me again at verse 18, **"On the same day <u>the Lord made</u> a covenant with Abram…"** The Bible does not say that Abraham made a covenant with God, but it says that the Lord is the One who made the covenant with him. That is an imposed covenant. We are going to come back to Genesis 15 but I want to show you several other Scriptures that have the same language.

Exodus 24:8 says, **"And Moses took the blood, sprinkled it on the people, and said, "This is the blood of the covenant which <u>the Lord has made</u> with you according to all these words.""**

Acts 3:25 says, **"You are sons of the prophets, and of the covenant which <u>God made</u> with our fathers, saying to Abraham, 'And in your seed all the families of the earth shall be blessed.'"**

Hebrews 8:10 says, **"For this is the covenant that <u>I will</u> <u>make</u> with the house of Israel after those days, says the Lord..."**

Hebrews 9:20 says, **Saying, "This is the blood of the covenant which <u>God has commanded you</u>.""**

Let's go back to Genesis 15 and look at some more things about this great experience that Abraham had. The story begins by Almighty God speaking to Abraham and telling him that He had made him the father of many nations, then in verse 6 it says, **"And <u>he believed</u> in the Lord, and He accounted it to him for righteousness."**

Galatians 3:6 says, **"Just as <u>Abraham believed</u> <u>God</u>, and it was accounted to him for righteousness."**

Romans 4:20, 21 says, **"He did not waver at the promise of God through unbelief, but was strengthened <u>in faith</u>, giving glory to God, and being <u>fully convinced</u> that what He had promised He was also able to perform."**

Do you see it? I am talking about Abraham's faith in God. The Lord told Abraham, in Romans 4:17, **"...I have made you a father of many nations..."** Abraham could not do this himself, only God could do it (which is grace); yet Abraham still had to believe or operate in faith so God could bring it to pass. God did not make him become a father of many nations. He could have rejected God's imposition, couldn't he? He could have rejected God's grace. Christians today do that all the time, it is called frustrating or setting aside the grace of God (Galatians 2:21). I am so glad Abraham chose to receive God's blessing or imposition. He chose to operate in faith, didn't he? When it comes to you and me, God is saying to us (in this Blood covenant) that I have already healed you (which is grace), but yet, many Christians respond to that by saying, "Well I sure don't feel or look healed!" That is not faith! If you say that, then you are rejecting and frustrating the grace of God in your life and thereby refusing your healing.

Whether you realize it or not, you are saying that you refuse to receive the blessings of God's covenant in your life. You need to say, "Father, I believe you and I receive that healing into my body right now, and I confess and declare that I am healed and healthy in Jesus' Name!" That is how you operate in faith for every area of your life. That is how you will experience and enjoy all of the blessings of this Blood covenant with God! I have said this before in some of my other books but it bears repeating. What God told Abraham was absolutely ridiculous and impossible for man to do, but not for God. God does the impossible! The Lord did not tell him that he was going to have just a big (5 to 10 children) family. Abraham and Sarah were not capable of having any children; yet the Lord said that they would not be able to count all their descendants.

Here is what amazes me; the Bible said that Abraham simply believed what God said! Something that astounding and mind boggling, and he just chose to believe God. <u>He just believed</u>! That is how simple it is to operate in faith. One of my books is entitled "**Just Believe**" and it is talking about how we as the Church need to get back to the simplicity of our faith in God. The Church today has made faith in God too complex, and we must get back to its simplicity. I hope you will go to our website and get the book. Faith is a decision that you make and it does not take six months to do that. You don't have to know everything about someone to make a decision to believe him. Even if he is lying to you, you can still choose to believe him. Sometimes people will say that they can't believe, but that is an incorrect statement. You can believe anything you want to believe whether it's true or not; the choice is yours.

When you read in II Corinthians 8:9 that Jesus became poor with your poverty, and in its place, has made you rich, you can choose to believe that immediately. If you say, "I can't believe that" then you are lying. You can believe it if you want to. If you say, "I can't believe that verse is true for me", you are actually saying I do not believe it, because you can believe anything you want to believe. According to Hebrews 11:1, the very nature of faith is to believe in what you do not see. Faith is the evidence of what you do not see. Listen! Every time you read something in the Bible that describes what Jesus did for you at Calvary, immediately say, "I believe that"! The choice is yours; so make the right choice! Remember Deuteronomy 30:19?

"I call heaven and earth as witnesses today against you, that I have set before you life and death, blessing and cursing; <u>therefore choose life</u>, that both you and your descendants may live."

The Lord made it very clear to us, didn't He? The choice is yours and the choice is mine. God did not ask for our opinion on this. He simply told us that in this world is life, death, blessing and cursing; but God loves us so much and He is so good to us that He told us which ones to choose. Notice though, He did not say that He would choose for us. That verse is God imposing upon His people, but not forcing His will upon them. God's imposition to us in this new covenant is always good and for our benefit. We serve a good God! A benevolent Father! He only wants good for you and me, so reach out by faith and choose His goodness!

I find it interesting in Genesis 15:8-10 that when Abraham asked the Lord how he would know that he would inherit the land, God's answer was for Abraham to enter into a blood covenant with Him. God's covenant was confirmation and evidence that God would do what He said. Now we know that Abraham did not have a Bible back then, because it had not yet been written. He did not have any verses from the Bible he could spiritually stand on in faith, so God entered into a blood covenant with him. The Lord chose the blood covenant as something Abraham could relate to, and that would remind him of God's promise. It also shows me how important this covenant was to God. It was the Lord's idea to implement this, and we already found out that it was His plan for man before Adam and Eve walked the earth.

God allowed Abraham to enter into a covenant that would be everlasting. The Lord would never break it! He cannot break it because He cannot lie! The Lord proceeded to tell Abraham some specific animals he needed to get, but it does not say that He told him what to do with them. By the language of Genesis 15:10, it seems that Abraham knew which ones to cut in two, down the middle. It appears that he already knew how to cut a covenant. Where did he get this knowledge?   Did he already have an understanding of blood covenants? Again, there is nothing in this story that says that God explained to him what to do with the animals.

I believe the knowledge Abraham had about blood covenants was handed down from Adam and Eve. In Genesis 3:21, it says that God made tunics of skin, and clothed them. Where did He get the skins? The logical answer would be from the animals He killed, and of course when they were killed blood was shed. This was probably where the first blood covenant was introduced to humanity. After the flood, Noah also knew to offer a blood sacrifice to the Lord (Genesis 9:20-21). So, the understanding of a blood covenant was handed down from generation to generation.

Now, let's go back to Abraham in Genesis 15:12, 17. After he prepared the animals and the sun was going down, God put him into a deep sleep. Why did He do that? Remember, we are still talking about an imposed covenant. The Lord was letting Abraham know that he did not have anything to do with the making of this covenant. In other words, God did not tell Abraham to get his attorney's and we will all sit down at a conference table and hash this thing out. The Lord did not ask Abraham for his opinion about anything. He did not ask him if he wanted to introduce some other blessings or curses into the covenant. In essence, God said, "This is the covenant that you can enter in with me, and here is what I will do for you." Abraham could have said, "No, I am not interested," and walked away, but he was smarter than that wasn't he? He chose to believe God.

Let me ask you this, "What do you choose to believe?" Do you choose to believe God? Did you know that having faith in God (Mark 9:23; 11:22) and operating in that faith is how you believe God? We need to learn to believe God for everything. The Lord gave us our measure of faith, so let's use it for everything. All you have to do is say, "Yes" to God's covenant and all His wonderful blessings! How do you say "Yes" and receive? Just like Jesus taught us in Mark 11:23 and 24. To believe God for something means to believe what you say will come to pass. Don't doubt in your heart but really believe. Also, it means to believe you receive from God when you pray. When you release your faith this way, you are believing God.

Then, God came down in the fire and smoke and passed through those pieces of flesh and blood, but Abraham did not pass through them, only God. This was an imposed Covenant. You may be thinking, "What is so important about knowing that it is an imposed covenant?" For me, it is the same as getting a revelation of what God's grace is all about. It is also the same as understanding why you are in Christ and why you have all the blessings of Heaven available to you.

If you don't get it yet, here is what I am saying. Nothing in this awesome covenant has to do with how holy you are, how intelligent you are, how good looking you are, what color you are, where you were born or how much money you have. In other words, all that the Lord has blessed us with in this new Blood covenant has nothing to do with our performances; it is totally based and established on Jesus' performance at Calvary. Our performances do not determine if God will bless us, He has already done that. Yes, we need to put works with our faith, but we are not doing that to get God to bless us. We are doing that to respond to what He has already done. That is how we release our faith and appropriate the blessings which are already ours.

The Lord doesn't heal and prosper us because of how many hours we pray or how many poor people we feed, or because of any other humanitarian things we do. God has already healed us, redeemed us and set us free because of the works of Jesus at Calvary. That was God's part, and it is called grace. Our part is simply to believe that and say thank you; that is called faith. All of our praying, fasting, reading, and giving should be a demonstration of our love for God, but these things should not be done with the attitude of trying to get God go do something for us. Our desire should be to show the Lord how much we love Him and how we want to be a blessing to others. Our faith or believing God simply responds to what He has already finished for us in Christ.

The Lord Jesus finished everything for you and me through all His sufferings and death and resurrection. The covenant was made between God and Jesus, and we got in on it through our faith in God; not by our performances. If you study the Word, you will see that even our faith is a free gift from God (Romans 12:3; II Corinthians 4:13; Ephesians 2:8, 9; Hebrews 12:2). All these Scriptures I just gave you were not written to make this book longer. I gave those to you hoping that you will look them up and spend time meditating on them. All we need to do now is learn how to operate in faith and access God's grace (Romans 5:2). Everything that is ours in this Blood covenant we can experience and enjoy if we would just learn to use our faith. This great covenant was God's idea, not ours. He came up with it and He put it into operation.

Please let me say this one more time so you don't misunderstand me. When I talk about performances, I want to make sure you understand that there was nothing you could do out of your human and fleshly efforts to have a right to participate in God's covenant. Jesus gave us the right (in Him) to participate in this great covenant! Now that we are in it, we have a responsibility to bear the fruits of righteousness and the fruit of the spirit, but these are to be outward demonstrations of what the Lord freely accomplished in our spirit through Jesus' precious (covenant) Blood. The reason we can live a holy life and please the Lord is because He has changed us from the inside out. Being changed on the inside is what the Apostle Paul taught us in the book of Romans, but bearing fruit to demonstrate the new man is what the Apostle James taught us in his book. You could say that Paul talked about and dealt with the root of man's problem and James addressed the fruit.

I want to show you another very important Scripture in the new covenant that confirms this imposed covenant. It is found in Ephesians 2:6.

"And raised us up together, and <u>made us sit</u> together in the heavenly places in Christ Jesus."

I did not make me to sit. You did not make me to sit. My good deeds are not why I get to sit. God made me to sit, He did it. He made me to sit at His right hand in His throne room in Christ! It is not based on anything I have done or accomplished! It is only based on what my covenant representative did for me. So, I like to remind the Lord of what He did for me. I like to say, "Father, this Blood covenant was your idea, not mine, and I am so thankful for your great idea! <u>You made</u> me to sit at your right hand in Christ. Through Jesus' death you killed and eliminated the old man that I was. Then, <u>You made</u> me alive together with Christ and <u>You made</u> me into a new man in Him. You resurrected me together with Him and <u>You made</u> me to sit in your throne room. None of this was about what I could or could not do. It was only about what Jesus, my covenant representative could and did do for me at Calvary. So, I now see that all I need to do every day is to just rest in Christ because You have done everything for me."

Think about this with me. God made me to sit in the Heavenly places in Christ. It is already finished! I am not trying to pray enough, read the Bible, go to church, feed the poor or fast enough so that God will seat me in His throne room. Our covenant Father loves you and me so much that He did it all for us, without asking us for our input. He did not ask us what we thought about His plan. He did not ask us if we had anything to add to it. He did it all for you and me in Christ. But, before we will experience all these wonderful blessings we have to accept His imposition. When you accept it, because God did a perfect work in Christ, expect to walk and live in the fullness of it.

One of the benefits of this Blood covenant is knowing that Jesus is our peace, and as the Lord told us in John 14:27, since He is our peace we will not let our heart be troubled or afraid about anything. Another Scripture to go with this is a Messianic prophecy about Jesus found in Isaiah 42:6.

"I, the Lord, have called You in righteousness, and will hold Your hand; I will keep You and give <u>You as a covenant to</u> <u>the people</u>, as a light to the Gentiles."

Wow! Jesus is our peace and <u>He is also our covenant!</u> We are not only in covenant with God in Christ, but our Lord and Savior is our covenant! Since Jesus is my peace and my covenant, He is my all sufficiency in every area of my life; therefore, I will never let me heart be troubled, afraid or worried about anything in Jesus' Name!! I will never lack or need anything because I am in covenant with Almighty God! I have abundance of supply and more than enough for me, my family and to do all God has called me to do! I am reigning as a king in life and I am a great blessing to others! I am also a huge financial channel that God is using to send His Gospel throughout the earth! It would be good if you would also make this same confession over yourself. You are in Christ (in Blood covenant with God). Believe it! Confess it! (Mark 11:23, 24; Job 22:28) And expect to experience it!

CHAPTER
4

AN UNCIRCUMCISED PHILISTINE

What is an uncircumcised philistine? I know in the Bible it refers to a Philistine who is not in covenant with God as Israel was, but what else does it mean? I believe it represents anything the devil brings against you in life. Any kind of sickness, disease, poverty, fear, lust, sin and evil is an uncircumcised Philistine. That means it is not part of our covenant with God, and since it is not in our covenant, it does not have any authority or power over us! We need to deal with it just like David dealt with Goliath! Don't give it any place in your life (Ephesians 4:27)! Do you remember the story, in I Samuel 17, of David's great victory? The Bible says this of David in verse 26:

"Then David spoke to the men who stood by him, saying, "What shall be done for the man who kills this Philistine and takes away the reproach from Israel? For who is this <u>uncircumcised Philistine</u>, that he should defy the armies of the living God?"" (Emphasis added throughout chapter).

Remember, even though David was a young man he still understood about covenant; especially blood covenant with God. We need to take a lesson here from David. Theologians tell us that Goliath may have been from nine to eleven feet tall and the armor he wore could have weighed up to 300 pounds. He was huge! You could say that he was a gigantic problem! Have you ever had any problems to deal with? You may be facing something coming against you right now. It could be a disease or great financial distress that seems like a Goliath in your life.

Whatever it may be, do not call it a Goliath, but address it the way David did. He called Goliath an uncircumcised Philistine. Say the same thing to whatever you are dealing with, call it an uncircumcised Philistine. By himself, David was no match for this monstrous warrior. David probably looked puny compared to Goliath. He was not dressed with any armor, and the only weapon he had was a sling shot. Naturally speaking, if this battle was only between David and Goliath, David would not have returned home that day. The good news is David was not alone in his confrontation with the giant. David revealed to us a wealth of information, really revelation, when he called Goliath an uncircumcised Philistine. There was more going on in the spirit realm than anyone could see in the natural realm.

David knew that Goliath was not circumcised. You could say that was "code" for describing someone or something without a covenant with God. By calling him uncircumcised he was saying, "God is not on your side, but He is on my side. I am actually not facing this battle by myself. I don't have to fight this giant by myself. My covenant God will fight for me!" That is why David said that the battle is the Lord's, and He will give you into our hands (I Samuel 17:47b)! David understood how to operate in faith and experience his blood covenant rights. He knew how to allow his covenant partner (Almighty God) to have access in his life and honor His part of the covenant with him. As you know, this was not the first time he called on his covenant partner.

Verse 37 in this same chapter says: **"Moreover David said," The Lord, who delivered me from the paw of the lion and from the paw of the bear, He will deliver me from the hand of this Philistine." And Saul said to David, "Go, and the Lord be with you!""**

We need to learn how to do the same thing in our lives today! Learn everything you can about your covenant with God, which involves your identity in Christ, and then aggressively expect to walk in all the benefits of it! If the power and protection of this blood covenant was not a reality in David's life he would have never been bold enough to face and defeat the lion and the bear. The great protection chapters of Psalm 23 and 91, describe the covenant rights of every Christian! Don't miss out on what belongs to you! Well, you may say, "I am waiting on God to move." Waiting on God to move is like having a bank account with $100,000 in it and then waiting on the president of the bank to bring you some money. If you don't move by making a withdrawal from the bank then you will wait forever and never enjoy any of your money! God has already moved! He moved about 2000 years ago through the death and resurrection of Jesus and finished everything for us! It is now <u>your move</u>!

You may ask, "How do I move?" You move in faith. When you release your faith by saying what you believe will come to pass (Mark 11:23, 24) you are moving just like David did. That is how you access, what I like to call your grace account, and receive what you need and desire. Let's read some more about David's amazing faith.

"So the Philistine came, and began drawing near to David, and the man who bore the shield went before him.

And when the Philistine looked about and saw David, he disdained him; for he was only a youth, ruddy and good-looking.

So the Philistine said to David, "Am I a dog, that you come to me with sticks?" And the Philistine cursed David by his gods.

And the Philistine said to David, "Come to me, and I will give your flesh to the birds of the air and the beasts of the field!"

Then David said to the Philistine, "You come to me with a sword, with a spear, and with a javelin. But I come to you in the name of the Lord of hosts, the God of the armies of Israel, whom you have defied.

This day the Lord will deliver you into my hand, and I will strike you and take your head from you. And this day I will give the carcasses of the camp of the Philistines to the birds of the air and the wild beasts of the earth, that all the earth may know that there is a God in Israel.

Then all this assembly shall know that the Lord does not save with sword and spear; for the battle is the Lord's, and He will give you into our hands."

So it was, when the Philistine arose and came and drew near to meet David, that David hurried and ran toward the army to meet the Philistine.

Then David put his hand in his bag and took out a stone; and he slung it and struck the Philistine in his forehead, so that the stone sank into his forehead, and he fell on his face to the earth.

So David prevailed over the Philistine with a sling and a stone, and struck the Philistine and killed him." (I Samuel 17:41-50a)

David knew that God made this blood covenant with him. Since it was His idea and everything written in it came from Him, then He would surely stand behind it. The same is true in our lives today. We are in an imposed covenant, and we do not make it work; God does. He did everything for us through the substitutionary sacrifice of Jesus. All we have to do is believe the Word of this covenant and obey it; then expect to see it work in our lives!

I hope you noticed in our story that David spoke to his problem, the uncircumcised Philistine, didn't he? He even ran toward Goliath and not away from him. He had such confidence in the integrity of the Word of the covenant, he ran towards his problem; not afraid to face it and deal with it! He knew that God would honor the covenant by defending him and giving him victory over the giant.

We need to get so established in the Word of God (the Word of our covenant) that when the devil attacks us, we immediately recognize that the problem (fear, sickness, pain, lack or whatever it may be) is an uncircumcised Philistine that needs to be slain and beheaded! Run towards the problem like David did, by boldly declaring what you expect to come to pass!

"The wicked flee when no one pursues, but the righteous are bold as a lion." (Proverbs 28:1)

The wicked flee, but not the righteous. Because of our covenant with God, we are His righteousness in Christ and we are bold as a lion! The way you spiritually run towards the problem is to be quick to speak to it, like David did, and tell it what its future is! David prophesied to that giant, didn't he? Right now, you need to prophesy to whatever uncircumcised Philistine is coming against you; whether it is in your life, marriage, job, ministry or children and command it to die and leave in Jesus' Name!! Let's make it a habit of always doing what God said in Job 22:28 (Amplified Bible).

"<u>You will also decide and decree a thing</u>, and it will be established for you; and the light [of God's favor] will shine upon your ways."

David told Goliath exactly what he was going to do to him. He did not say it sheepishly or nervously but boldly and with great confidence! He had faith in God! He really believed that he was in a blood covenant with the Creator! He believed so much in the validity of his covenant with God that he was willing to risk his life that day! Even though this was true of David, I don't think he believed that what he was doing put his life at risk. I am talking about what he really believed in his heart. I don't think the thought occurred to him that he might die. I believe that he had such a great revelation of his covenant with God and what it meant to have God as his covenant partner that he did not see his life at risk. Despite how massive Goliath (the problem) was, the greatness and superiority of David's covenant partner totally overshadowed and completely dominated the giant's presence. You may be thinking, "I did not see all that when I read this story." You can only see that through your eyes of faith, and that only comes by spending time in the Word. I am talking about giving the Holy Spirit time, through daily discipline, to build up your faith in what it means to be in Blood covenant with God.

Now, if you think about what I just said concerning the courage of David, it probably describes the apex or pinnacle of his faith! He did not have any fear! He was so totally convinced and assured that God would honor His covenant Word in his life that he was not thinking about himself at all. His mind was on God, his covenant partner, and God's mind was on his covenant partner (David). David saw an enemy verbally attacking and coming against his covenant partner (God) and came to offer his assistance.

Remember, in a blood covenant, whatever is mine is available to you (my covenant partner) with all my abilities and resources. I am here for you and you are here for me! David was quick to fight Goliath to honor his covenant partnership with God. So, David went onto the battle field expecting to see his covenant partner vindicated and glorified! I believe that describes what was on his mind. We need to believe and operate the same way, as God's covenant partners, when it comes to resisting the devil. He is God's enemy and our enemy! Our covenant partner wants to use us everywhere we go in demonstrating the devil's defeat and setting free those who are bound by him! Let's go do it in Jesus' Name! Let's go win the lost to Jesus and see God's Kingdom established in the hearts of men!

Now, there is another verse in this story (1 Samuel17:29) that I believe you will understand better after gaining more knowledge about this Blood covenant, **"And David said, "What have I done now? Is there not a cause?""** Can you see that he was saying, "Don't we have a reason to stand up and fight? This uncircumcised Philistine is not only attacking us but he is coming against our covenant partner (God)!" If someone attacks your covenant partner, what do you do? Bury your head in the sand? Run away in fear? No!! You go to your partners rescue and do everything you can to assist and help! That is what blood covenant partners do!

We have a reason to fulfill all that God has called us to do! We have a reason to be bold and to live by faith! We have a reason to experience our healing, all the blessings of the Lord in our lives, all of our bills paid, a successful marriage, a happy family and total peace of mind! We have a reason to finance and preach this Gospel throughout the entire world! We serve the Lord God Almighty and He is our covenant partner, and we are here to get a job done for Him, and there is not any enemy who can defeat us! No one can defeat us because no one can defeat our covenant partner!

Here is another New Testament Scripture you can now look at in the light of our Blood covenant.

"But seek first the kingdom of God and His righteousness, and all these things shall be added to you." (Matthew 6:33)

Couldn't you say that David was seeking God's Kingdom and His righteousness first when he went out to fight Goliath? When he said, "Is there not a cause", he was saying that there should be a reason for us to stand up to this man. Aren't we here to see God's will done in our lives? Seeking God's righteousness is seeking for God's way of doing things to be fulfilled on the earth. Therefore, seeking first the Kingdom of God and His righteousness is honoring our covenant partner, isn't it? The phrase, "All these things shall be added to you" is God's part in honoring His covenant partners (Believers).

When we release our faith by believing and obeying God's covenant Word then He will honor His part of the covenant in our lives. He will bring to pass all that Jesus did for us through His covenant Blood! So, I want to encourage you to believe it and expect to see it work in your life! You have covenant rights!! The devil is an uncircumcised Philistine, aggressively resist him and tell him to get out of your life and family in Jesus' Name!

Look with me now in Joshua chapter nine, it talks about how the Gibeonites deceived the Israelites into entering into a covenant with them (verse 15). Even though God would have warned them of the deception they chose not to ask counsel of the Lord (verse 14). In chapter ten, we are told that five kings of the Amorites came against the Gibeonites (who were now in covenant with Israel). So, they immediately asked their covenant partners for help. Even though the children of Israel had been tricked into this covenant, it was still a real covenant and they felt obligated to honor it. Joshua 10: 8 says:

"And the Lord said to Joshua, "Do not fear them (the five kings), **for I have delivered them into your hand; not a man of them shall stand before you.""**

Now watch this. First, Joshua and the children of Israel came to the rescue of their covenant partners (the Gibeonites), and then Almighty God came to the rescue of his covenant partners (the Israelites), after they engaged in battle with the five kings! Always expect your Blood covenant partner (El Shaddai- the all sufficient One) to be there for you! He said that He will never leave us nor forsake us (Hebrews 13:5)! He is not only with us as He was with Israel, but He also lives in us, and this covenant union is something we are going to talk more about in another chapter.

The next time you read this story you will see just how much God was with His covenant people.

For example, while Joshua and his men were engaged in battle, Joshua realized that he needed more daylight to fight, so he did something that can only be done by a person in covenant with God. What he did was what only God could do, and the only reason he could expect the Lord to do it was because of his covenant partnership with Him. Think about that! Almighty God is your covenant partner; therefore, the phrase "I can't" should never be in your vocabulary! "I am afraid" is another phrase that should never be in your vocabulary; as well as the poverty-stricken words "I cannot afford that".

Only the Word of God's covenant should be in your vocabulary. I can do all things through Christ Jesus who strengthens me is covenant talk, and should always be your normal language. Proverbs 18:21 says that **death and life are in the power of the tongue.** Guard your mouth every day and make sure your language is covenant language! It is very important to spend time learning how to speak the Word of God, but also spend time thinking about and meditating on who your covenant partner is and what He has made available to you. Now listen to what a man in covenant with God can do.

"Then Joshua spoke to the Lord in the day when the Lord delivered up the Amorites before the

children of Israel, and he said in the sight of Israel: "Sun, stand still over Gibeon; and Moon, in the Valley of Aijalon."

So the sun stood still, and the moon stopped, till the people had revenge upon their enemies.

"And there has been no day like that, before it or after it, that the Lord heeded the voice of a man; for <u>the Lord fought</u> for <u>Israel</u>."

God created the Sun, moon, Earth, planets and all the solar systems, didn't He? God did that, but yet a man (a covenant man) could step out in faith and command something that Almighty God created, to obey him, and it did! Even though Joshua did not understand that the Earth rotates around the Sun, the Lord still honored his command (Isaiah 45:11). Do you want to know how powerful your covenant is? God used a man, just like He can use you and me, to speak some faith filled words, and stop the Earth from rotating around the Sun, so that it looked like the Sun stood still for almost a whole day! We don't know what all God did to keep the Earth from crashing into the Sun, but that was not Joshua's responsibility.

As you read this story and stand amazed at what God can do through one of His children who will just dare to step out in faith and put a demand on his covenant; always remember that we are in a better covenant than Joshua was in! Since God could do that through Joshua in the old covenant, what can He do through you and me in this new Blood covenant; ratified by the Blood of the Son of God? The answer is Mark 9:23, **"Jesus said to him, "If you can believe, all things are possible to him who believes."** What the Lord did through Joshua is just one of the "all things" He can do through any covenant Believer who will have faith in God and say what he believes in his heart will come to pass! Before we move on, don't forget what else Joshua's covenant partner did that day.

"And it happened, as they fled before Israel and were on the descent of Beth Horon, that <u>the Lord cast down large</u> <u>hailstones</u> from heaven on them as far as Azekah, and they died. There were more who died from the hailstones than the children of Israel killed with the sword." (Joshua 10:11)

The Lord definitely fought for Israel! You may be thinking, "I wish He would fight for me like that." I want you to know that He already has, at a place called Calvary. I believe that the greatest demonstration of God's power was not at creation, not at the parting of the Red Sea, not when Joshua spoke to the Sun, not when Jesus walked on the water, but it was when God the Father raised Jesus from the dead! If you think about it, all of hell was trying to stop that miracle from coming to pass. The devil and his demons did not want that to happen, but they could not do a thing to stop it!

According to Ephesians chapter one, that same unlimited resurrection power is in you (as a Spirit-filled Believer) today! It is just one of the benefits you have in this new covenant. We have so much more now than David and Joshua had in the old covenant! Remember, they were not born again or filled with the Spirit. They were not God's righteousness in Christ. They did not have the Name or the Blood of Jesus, and they did not have the whole armor of God to wear; yet, look at all the great miracles God did for them through that old covenant. If they could release their faith back then and put such a great demand on their covenant with God, how much more we, as new covenant Believers, should be able to release our faith and receive from God today!

I want us to look at another person who had great faith in God and His covenant. Jonathan was a man who completely relied and depended on his covenant with God. He and his armorbearer decided one day to go over to the Philistine garrison and engage in battle with them, only trusting the Lord to give them the victory. I Samuel 14:6 says:

"Then Jonathan said to the young man who bore his armor, "Come, let us go over to the garrison of these <u>uncircumcised</u>; it may be that the Lord will work for us. For nothing restrains the Lord from saving by many or by few.""

Please let me remind you that a garrison can have anywhere from a few thousand to well over 60,000 men. So, on the Philistine's side there may have been from 2000 to 60,000 men, but on Jonathan's side there were only two. Naturally speaking, I would say that they were very much outnumbered, wouldn't you? Even though that was true, in Jonathan's mind, like David's, that was not a problem. When you have a reality of what it means to be in covenant with Almighty God, you always know that the majority is on your side! God is always the majority! Let me share with you how I know this blood covenant was a fully established reality in Johnathan's life. Obviously, the end results are the best evidence, but there is something else I want you to see.

He called the Philistines, the <u>uncircumcised</u>. That one word tells me that he knew that God was not fighting for the Philistines, but He was fighting for him and his armorbearer. Jonathan had such great confidence that God (his covenant partner) would come through for him that he was willing do what militarily seemed ignorant and ridiculous. Look with me at some verses here.

"Then Jonathan said, "Very well, let us cross over to these men, and we will show ourselves to them.

If they say thus to us, 'Wait until we come to you,' then we will stand still in our place and not go up to them.

But if they say thus, 'Come up to us,' then we will go up. For the Lord has delivered them into our hand, and this will be a sign to us." (I Samuel 14:8-10)

The only tactical advantage Jonathan had, since they were hugely outnumbered, was the element of surprise; and as you just read, that was the first thing they gave away. It seemed that they thought giving away their position and having the Philistines come to them or vice versa would be a sign from God of their impending victory. In essence, they were saying, "We will just wait right here for them to come to us or if they want us to come to them, then we will go up the mountain. Either way, we will wait to see what they want to do." Voluntarily waiting for your enemy to come to you or choosing to go to them, while knowing they are fully aware of what you are doing, was definitely not what we would call guerilla warfare or a wise tactical decision. No military person in his right mind would think that way, unless he knew what it meant to be in covenant with God.

When you are in covenant with the Lord and your believing and thinking are consumed with God's covenant Word, then no problem, no sickness, no financial lack, no fear and no mountain will seem too big to you! Nothing will seem like the odds are against you because you are not considering how things appear in the natural realm! Remember, Abraham did not consider his own body when he was about 100 years old. He only considered what his covenant partner said.

Jonathan was the same way. He knew the Philistines had more men than he did, but his natural vision was not what he was relying on. He was looking at the situation through his eyes of faith. He saw how big and great his covenant partner was, so everything else around him looked small and insignificant. He didn't care how many men were on that mountain, he knew he could take it and overcome his enemy because he had faith in the integrity of his covenant partner! He believed in the faithfulness of God, and he knew that the Lord would not let him down!

We need to get into the Word of God and expect the Lord to develop our faith just as strong in our covenant walk with God! I really like what Johnathan said at the end of verse 6, **"...For nothing restrains the Lord from saving by many or by few."** That is a great covenant statement! It's very important that you believe in your heart that the amount of people on your side is irrelevant. Also, it doesn't matter how many are against you, it doesn't matter what the doctor says, it doesn't matter how big the debt is, it doesn't matter how your spouse and children are acting and it doesn't matter what's going on in the economy, settle it in your heart and mind that you will not be discouraged by those natural problems! Yes, they are real, but God is real to and He is greater than those difficulties! Rest and rely on the fact that you know that the creator of the universe is your covenant partner! You know that He knows no restraint in your life, which means He knows no limit in what He can do for you! There is not anything too hard for God to do in you and through you for others in the covenant Name of Jesus! Now let's read the rest of the story and see what God did for Johnathan and his armorbearer.

"Then the men of the garrison called to Jonathan and his armorbearer, and said, "Come up to us, and we will show you something." Jonathan said to his armorbearer, "Come up after me, for the Lord has delivered them into the hand of Israel."

And Jonathan climbed up on his hands and knees with his armor bearer after him; and they fell before Jonathan. And as he came after him, his armorbearer killed them.

That first slaughter which Jonathan and his armorbearer made was about <u>twenty men within about half an acre of</u> <u>land</u>.

And there was trembling in the camp, in the field, and among all the people. The garrison and the raiders also trembled; and the earth quaked, so that it was a very great trembling." (I Samuel 14:12-15)

The Bible said that Johnathan climbed up the mountain and fought the Philistines on his hands and knees and they killed twenty men within about half an acre. Wow! That was an awesome victory! I don't know anyone who can kill twenty men in battle within half an acre while standing on their feet, much less while on their hands and knees ascending a mountain. This story of faith in God is a great example of trusting God for deliverance, healing and provision; despite the overwhelming odds against you. Their situation looked totally bleak and hopeless, but like David, they were not moved by the threat coming against them, they were only moved by their faith in God. I want to encourage you to stand up boldly on your covenant with the Lord! Don't let the devil (your enemy) talk you out of any of your covenant rights! As I have said before, the devil is an uncircumcised Philistine and it doesn't matter what he is bringing against you, God will cause you to triumph over it all (II Corinthians 2:14)!

Be quick to use your spiritual weapons! You have been given a great arsenal (the Name of Jesus, the Blood of Jesus, the gifts of the Spirit, the whole armor of God and others)! As we have seen in this chapter, Joshua, David and Johnathan were champions of faith, weren't they? Why were they champions of faith? Was it because of their natural talents and abilities? No, it was because of their faith in God and the relationship they had with Him through the blood covenant.

I hope you will start declaring this over your life, **"I am a champion of faith through my covenant with God! Father I trust you as my one and only source of supply! I will never be afraid or troubled about anything because you are my covenant partner and you are always there for me! Thank you, Father, that you know no limit in my life. There isn't anything too hard for you to do for me, and through me for others! You can save by many or by few, so it doesn't matter how things look in the natural realm! I will always win and I will always triumph in Jesus' Name!"**

CHAPTER
5

"EAT MY FLESH AND DRINK MY BLOOD"
What Did Jesus Mean By That?

Do you think the statement you just read in the title of this chapter has something to do with a blood covenant? If you are not sure, please read chapter two in this book again. If you read that verse in John chapter six, where the Lord talked about eating His flesh and drinking His Blood, for the first time, without an understanding of God's Blood covenant and our identification with Christ, you would probably be very alarmed. So, let me begin by saying that the Bible is not talking about cannibalism here. Jesus was simply using a very descriptive way to emphasize our union with Him, and to show how **one** we are with Him in this new Blood covenant.

I praise the Lord for the precious Blood of Jesus, for the blood of animals doesn't even compare! There was no redemption in the blood of animals, but there is eternal redemption and the forgiveness of sins in the Blood of Jesus! Jesus' Blood is covenant Blood, isn't it? I also praise the Lord for the offering and sacrifice of His entire being for you and me! He truly was the ultimate and supreme sacrifice for man! By what He suffered at Calvary, He proved to us how much He loves the Father and how much He loves you and me. Therefore, I want to know Him and experience greater and deeper intimacy with Him every day. I also want to know and understand everything I can about His substitutionary sacrifice for me! I hope that you feel the same way.

You may not realize it, but what I just shared with you in the last few sentences, is the key to revival in the Church today. In case you are still thinking about what those sentences were which relate to revival, I will sum it up for you. When Christians make time in their busy schedules to get to know the Lord better, when they make time to learn their identity in Christ and then when they go out and witness and minister the love and power of God to the people, you will see revival in the Church. Now, the result of revival in the hearts of Believers will be supernatural evangelism spreading throughout every town and city in every nation.

Revival is for Christians and evangelism is for the Lost. When the Church is truly revived in their identity in Christ then we will see multitudes of the lost won to Jesus and Christians trained and discipled throughout the world! Whenever you get a chance, I hope you will go on Youtube and listen to the 25 audio messages entitled "Have You Found Yourself". Just type in "Dwayne Norman Have You Found Yourself" and you will see parts 1 through 25, and you will also see a picture of my book "IN CHRIST-True Purpose, True Peace, True Fulfillment".

Let's go ahead and look at some powerful things that the Lord said in John 6:47-58.

"Most assuredly, I say to you, he who believes in Me has everlasting life.

I am the bread of life.

Your fathers ate the manna in the wilderness, and are dead.

This is the bread which comes down from heaven, that one may eat of it and not die.

I am the living bread which came down from heaven. If anyone eats of this bread, he will live forever; and the bread that I shall give is My flesh, which I shall give for the life of the world.

The Jews therefore quarreled among themselves, saying, "How can this Man give us His flesh to eat?"

Then Jesus said to them, "Most assuredly, I say to you, <u>unless you eat the flesh of the Son of Man and drink His blood, you have no life in you</u>.

<u>Whoever eats My flesh and drinks My blood has eternal life</u>, and I will raise him up at the last day.

For My flesh is food indeed, and My blood is drink indeed.

He who eats My flesh and drinks My blood abides in Me, and I in him.

As the living Father sent Me, and I live because of the Father, so he who feeds on Me will live because of Me.

This is the bread which came down from heaven-not as your fathers ate the manna, and are dead. He who eats this bread will live forever." (Emphasis added throughout chapter)

It is important to remember that when Jesus talked about eating His flesh and drinking His Blood, the Jews listening to His message already had some understanding about blood covenants. They knew about the covenant meal and the binding relationship between covenant partners. Yet, they were still shocked at how He chose to describe the identification and union between these covenant partners. They had never heard it explained that way. This teaching was new and very revolutionary to them, and they could not make sense of it. The reason it was unfamiliar to them was because Jesus was sharing deeper knowledge and revelation than was available for unregenerate man to understand at that time, since they were still in the old covenant.

The Lord was describing the oneness and total union that's made real in the life of every person who becomes a new creation in Christ (II Corinthians

5:17)! No one could experience this kind of union with the Lord Jesus until after He died and arose from the dead. The Lord was sharing an awesome truth about the new birth experience that those listening to the message at that time could not receive. They could not grasp the depth of what He said. He was actually introducing the reality of a new Blood covenant that would soon replace the old one. They could choose to believe what He said, but they could not experience the full reality of it. That can only be experienced in Christ.

In the Lord's message, He talks about the manna that God rained down on the children of Israel, and then describes Himself as the living bread sent from Heaven. Let me remind you of what God said about Israel in the wilderness.

"All ate the same spiritual food, and all drank the same spiritual drink. For they drank of that spiritual Rock that followed them, and that Rock was Christ." (I Corinthians 10:3-4)

Even after Israel crossed the Red Sea, their spiritual food and drink was symbolic of Christ, and Jesus confirms that in John chapter six by describing Himself as the bread of life which came down from Heaven. So, for Israel, the water they drank and the bread they ate represented Jesus strengthening and sustaining them every day. You could say that all their life came from Him. When the Lord said to eat

His flesh and drink His Blood, He was also talking about the same thing. He is our strength and sustenance, but there was something else He was talking about that no one in the old covenant could receive. I believe that Jesus looked forward to the day (Hebrews 12:2) when He could come live inside of you and me through the person of the Holy Spirit and we could become **one** with Him. This is mainly what He was referring to in John 6:56 when He said:

"He who eats My flesh and drinks My blood abides in Me, and I in him."

Let me give you a simple example. In your mind, picture me holding a cheese burger in my hand, and you can clearly see both the cheeseburger and me. You could say that I am separated from that burger, can't you? That is, it is not in me or part of me yet. I am not one with the cheeseburger, am I? As long as it is in my hand it is not inside of me. How do I become one with the cheeseburger? What do I need to do? I need to <u>eat it,</u> don't I? If it's a glass of water I'm holding then I need to drink it. The process of eating and drinking it is how I become one with it. It is how the burger and I come into union with each other. Now, once I eat it, it becomes part of me, doesn't it? You will not see the cheese burger anymore. We have become one with each other. But now listen, the way I experienced that union with the cheese burger is when I ate it.

When I teach Believers what it means to be in Christ, I like to bring out the point that since I am in Christ, I am no longer by myself. As Galatians 2:20 says in the King James translation, **"...Nevertheless I live; yet not I, but <u>Christ liveth in me</u>..."** Please pay close attention here! There is no such thing as Dwayne Norman apart from Christ! Yes, it's true that Dwayne Norman without Christ can't do anything and does not have anything, but that Dwayne Norman does not exist anymore!

Remember that cheese burger that I ate? It does not exist by itself any longer; it became one with me. We are completely united with each other. Yes, it's true; you can talk about what that cheese burger was like before it became one with me, but that part of the cheese burger's life is over with isn't it? It's not just a cheese burger anymore; it has been joined with me. We are now one. Can you see this? Now, think about your identification with Christ. It is not just about you anymore. You have been "swallowed up" in Christ! Can you see how strong and secure you union is with Jesus? You both are **one** with each other!

Of course, I remember what it was like without Jesus, and I praise God and give Him all the glory for all that He delivered me from, but my old life is dead and gone! I don't dwell on that anymore! The Bible doesn't tell me to focus my attention everyday on who I used to be, but it does tell me to acknowledge (confess and focus my attention on) every good thing in me in Christ (Philemon 1:6)! It is all about my oneness with Jesus from now on. It is no longer about my old identity before my union with Christ. My old identity is not my identity anymore! I now have a **new identity** in Christ! You need to get a vision of how God sees you now, in Christ and in Blood covenant with Him! My life now is not just about me, but Christ liveth in me; that's who I am forever! As the Apostle Paul said, **"For to me, to live is Christ, and to die is gain."** (Philippians 1:21)

When Jesus said, **"He who eats My flesh and drinks My blood abides in Me, and I in him"**, He was declaring the answer to what He prayed for in John 17:21-23.

"That they all may be one, as You, Father, are in Me, and I in You; that they also may be one in Us, that the world may believe that You sent Me.

And the glory which You gave Me I have given them, that they may be one just as We are one:

I in them, and You in Me; that they may be made perfect in one, and that the world may know that You have sent Me, and have loved them as You have loved Me."

We are now **one** with Jesus as He was with the Father! If you notice in this prayer, Jesus did not spend time talking about who He was without the Father. He dwelt on His oneness with the Father.

That is what His mind was on. That is what He was always conscience of everywhere He went. He knew that He wasn't by Himself, and He did not spend time thinking about that. He was consumed with His union with the Father and pleasing Him. He thought the Father's thoughts; He spoke the Father's Words. He heard His voice and He carried out His will. So, when He did all the great healings and miracles, it truly was the works of the Father through him. The reality and consciousness of His union with the Father enabled Him to be a completely yielded vessel for the will of God to be done.

The same is true for you and me today. We should always be dwelling on our abiding oneness with the risen Christ, seated in Him in the Heavenly places (Colossians 3:1-2)! If we are constantly dwelling on who we are without Christ then we will not be yielded vessels for the anointing of the Holy Spirit to flow through. But, when you are always acknowledging and meditating on your union with Christ and what it means to be in a Blood covenant with God, then your mind will be on all the attributes, qualities and blessings of your covenant partner and what He has done for you. So, when God gives you directions on what He wants you to do, you will be ready to carry them out without delay. You will be strong in faith and will have great expectancy in how He's going to use you for His glory!

Let me give you another good confession that will greatly enhance your spiritual life. Start talking to Jesus the same way He talked to the Father in John chapter 17. You could begin by saying, "Lord Jesus, because of this Blood covenant I am in with my Father through union with you, I am now **one** with You. I am in You and You are in me; therefore, the Father in You is now in me, and I am also the temple of the Holy Spirit. The glory the Father gave You, You have given to me so that we can be **one** and that the world may know that You have sent me to represent You in all that I say and do in Jesus' Name. Thank You Father for using me more and more in winning the lost to Jesus and in making disciples everywhere I go." I hope that you will believe and declare this in your life on a regular basis.

God also uses the union between a husband and wife to demonstrate the union between Christ and the Church. Marriage between a man and a woman is a good example of our covenant union with Christ. As Christians, my wife and I are one spirit with each other in Christ (I Corinthians 6:17), and because we are married (not just living together), the Bible says that in God's eyes we are one flesh. It also says that becoming one flesh is a great mystery and is compared to Christ and the Church (Ephesians 5:30-32).

Think about that for a moment. Even though I can be standing next to my wife, seeing both of us together, yet two different people; in God's eyes He sees us as one flesh. We may see two "flesh", but the Lord sees only one; there's the difference. If we don't see ourselves (husband and wife) as the Lord sees us then we will have problems in our marriage. You will not love your wife as Jesus loves the church and treat her like you treat your own body if you do not have an understanding and reality of your union (oneness) with her. When you really believe that you are one flesh with your wife, I mean really believe it, then you will not desire to do anything to hurt her or displease her, because you know that it would be the same thing as hurting yourself. You don't want to hurt yourself, so you don't want to hurt your wife. You always want to please yourself, so you should always want to please your wife as well. The same is true between Christ and the Church.

The greater understanding and reality we have of our Blood covenant with God, which also describes our union (oneness) with Christ, the more we will want to know and please Him. This entrance of God's Word into our lives will move us to press into and expect deeper intimacy and fellowship with the Lord. Sin will not be something we pursue or desire at all! We will not want to do anything to displease our Heavenly Father! Our hearts cry will be to know God better and to fulfill His will in our lives!

CHAPTER
6

THE COVENANT MEAL

Now, I want to show you how communion fits so beautifully in with what Jesus said about eating His flesh and drinking His Blood.   I Corinthians 11:23-25 say:

"For I received from the Lord that which I also delivered to you: that the Lord Jesus on the same night in which He was betrayed took bread;
And when He had given thanks, He broke it and said, Take, eat; this is My body which is broken for you; do this in remembrance of Me.
In the same manner He also took the cup after supper, saying, "This cup is the new covenant in My blood.   This do, as often as you drink it, in remembrance of Me.""

Partaking of communion is a great way to remind us of our union with Christ through reminding us of our Blood covenant with God. The covenant meal was a very important part of the covenant made between two people.   It was a confirmation to them that they were now covenant partners. As Christians, every time we partake of the Lord's Supper (or Table) we are reminded of Jesus' sufferings and His death and resurrection, which in turn focuses our attention once again on our oneness with the Lord.   It continually reminds us of our covenant partnership with Almighty God! What a wonderful way to bring these Truths back to our remembrance! **"For as often as you eat this bread and drink this cup, you proclaim the Lord's death till He comes."** (I Corinthians 11:26)

The Lord Jesus said to take communion in remembrance of Him, didn't He? What does the word "remembrance" mean? Does it mean to try to recall something that happened a long time ago, to see if you can remember some bits and pieces of a great event that took place about 2,000 years ago? That way you can say, "Oh yeah, I remember that." Obviously, the answer is no.   There is more to remembering Jesus' death and resurrection than we have been practicing.   In W. E. Vine's Expository Dictionary of New Testament Words, he defines remembrance as,

"In memory of but in an affectionate calling of the Person Himself to mind, not simply an external bringing to remembrance, but an awakening of mind."

In other words, using our hearts and minds and seeing all over again how Jesus represented you and me and all that He suffered to obtain our eternal redemption. Partaking of communion is a way for Believers to spiritually awake to everything that Jesus finished for us and blessed us with at Calvary. It is recognizing that all the events of the substitutionary sacrifice of Jesus are still a reality in our lives today! It is taking time to remind ourselves of who we are in Christ and what we have in Him, and that our Blood covenant with God is just as real in our lives now as it was when the Father made it with His Son in eternity past! We don't see the finished work of Christ as just something that transpired in the past and is over with, <u>but we see the work that Jesus did for us as a past completed work that has present finished results</u>!! What the Lord completed for us almost 2,000 years ago will be demonstrated and will work in our lives through out eternity!

Here is something else (through communion) that will help you to keep Jesus' death and resurrection a reality in your life, as well as a constant reminder of your union with Him. As we just read in I Corinthians 11:24 & 25, the Lord said to take, eat; this is My body and He said that this cup is the new covenant in My Blood. Most ministers, when they administer the bread and wine (or grape juice) in communion, they will start by saying that this bread "symbolizes or represents" Jesus' body and this juice "symbolizes or represents" His Blood.

Let me ask you this. Did Jesus say to take and eat this bread because it "represents" My body? Did He say that this bread and wine "symbolize" My body and Blood? Is that the way He said it? Look with me one more time at those two Scriptures. Jesus said, **"Take, eat; this is My body..."** and He said, **"This cup is the new covenant in My blood..."**

Now, I am not teaching transubstantiation here, and I know that you are probably aware of a very large denomination that teaches that. The ministers in that particular denomination believe that the bread and wine actually become the body and Blood of the Lord. Yet, the Bible does not teach that. Let's make sure what we teach agrees with God's Word and not man's religious and denominational ideas.

Please think about this with me. When Jesus served the elements of communion to His disciples, He knew that the bread in His hand did not transform into His body because He was using His body to present the bread to them. They were looking at the physical body of Christ presenting them with the bread, weren't they? The bread and His body were two different things, and the wine did not transform into His Blood. Here is where we are going to lose some Christians who don't know how to walk and live by faith.

I am talking about Christians who treat the elements of communion only as something that affects them in the natural realm; almost in a superstitious way. They talk about the bread and the wine as if they are some type of spiritual talisman or rabbit's foot to bring them good luck. They act like the bread and wine are some type of mystical, magical potions from God, so that all you have to do is eat them for some supernatural things to take place. They are not releasing any faith in the finished works of Christ. To these Christians, it is all about what they are physically (or outwardly) doing and not spiritually (inwardly) doing. They don't have a reality of what the bread and wine stand for and how to release their faith when they partake of these elements.

When we partake of the bread and wine, we need to do it in faith. We need to believe that the bread we are eating is the body of Jesus (even though it is not) and we need to believe that the wine or juice is His Blood (even though it is not). It's about faith in Jesus and His finished works! Do you remember when Jesus said to eat His flesh and drink His Blood? Once again, He wasn't talking about eating His physical flesh or drinking His physical blood.

Let me share with you what I like to do when I take the Lord's Supper. I take the bread in my hand and then in faith say, "Lord Jesus, I believe (faith) that I am eating your body (or flesh) as You told me to. I believe that as I eat Your body I am receiving into my body all of the perfect health, life and strength that's in Yours, and I declare that I am totally healed by Your 39 stripes!" It is about what you believe! Can you see that communion is a good way to release your faith and receive the healing Jesus already obtained for you?

After I release my faith in the bread, I do the same thing with the juice. By partaking this way in faith, I am making communion a very effective spiritual activity in my life! I then take the wine or juice and in faith I may say, "Lord Jesus, I believe that as I drink this juice I am drinking your sinless, redeeming and covenant Blood into myself. I believe that I am drinking into me all the resurrection life, power and prosperity in Your Blood and it is saturating every area of my life! Thank you for this awesome new covenant that I am in with You, the Holy Spirit and my Father God through Your precious Blood!" I hope that will give you a little bit of a guide line of some things you can confess when you take the Lord's Supper. By doing that, the revelation of your union with Jesus becomes even stronger within you. Well, there is still more we need to see about Communion in I Corinthians 10:16-21.

"The cup of blessing which we bless, is it not the <u>communion</u> of the blood of Christ? The bread which we break, is it not the <u>communion</u> of the body of Christ?

For we, though many, are one bread and one body; for <u>we all partake</u> of that one bread.

Observe Israel after the flesh: Are not those who eat of the sacrifices partakers of the altar?

What am I saying then? That an idol is anything, or what is offered to idols is anything?

Rather, that the things which the Gentiles sacrifice they sacrifice to demons and not to God, and I do not want you to have fellowship with demons.

You cannot drink the cup of the Lord and the cup of demons; you cannot partake of the Lord's table and of the table of demons." (Emphasis added through out chapter)

First of all, I like the way the Holy Spirit describes the Lord's Supper as "the cup of blessing", because taking the bread and the wine in faith and understanding will result in great blessings in your life. He talked about the communion of the Blood of Christ and the body of Christ. The word "communion" means to fellowship with, participate in and to partake of. Once again, as I have already brought out, God wants us to expect to partake of all that is in the body and Blood of Jesus when we take the elements. The only way to do that is by faith in God and in the finished works of Christ. Listen to how I Corinthians 10:16 reads in the Amplified Bible.

"The cup of blessing [of wine at the Lord's Supper] upon which we ask [God's] blessing, does it

not mean [that in drinking it] we participate in and share a fellowship (a communion) in the blood of Christ (the Messiah)? The bread which we break, does it not mean [that in eating it] we participate in and share a fellowship (a communion) in the body of Christ?"

If you noticed in these verses (I Corinthians 10:16-21), Paul gives us an example of how Israel operated after the flesh to illustrate a very important point we need to see today. He said that when they eat of the sacrifices, they are partaking (communion-fellowship) of the altar. What does that mean? At the altar is where their idol is set up and where they offer their sacrifice. When they eat of the food offered to that idol, they are actually engaging in a spiritual activity and having communion or fellowship with demons. Yes, the idol is just an inanimate object, it's not alive, but because they believe they can participate with evil spirits through the offering of their sacrifices, they open up a door in their lives for demonic activity. So, Paul says that what they are sacrificing is not a sacrifice to the idol but actually to demons, and he says they are drinking the cup of demons.

If they can have fellowship and a supernatural experience with demon spirits through sacrificing to a dumb idol, only because they believe; how much more can we have fellowship and a great supernatural experience with the Lord Jesus through the bread and wine of communion when we believe! There is one more thing I want us to look at concerning the Lord's Supper. It's found in I Corinthians 11:27-31.

"**Therefore whoever eats this bread or drinks this cup of the Lord in <u>an unworthy manner</u> will be guilty of the body and blood of the Lord.**

But let a man examine himself, and so let him eat of the bread and drink of the cup.

For he who eats and drinks in an unworthy manner eats and drinks judgment to himself, <u>not discerning the Lord's</u> body.

For this reason many are weak and sick among you, and many sleep.

For if we would <u>judge ourselves</u>, we would not be judged."

I grew up in a denominational church and was basically taught that if you had any sin in your life, don't take the Lord's Supper or something bad might happen to you. First of all, the purpose for taking communion is to remind yourself of all Jesus did for you at Calvary, and to remind yourself that you can receive forgiveness of any sins you may have committed. When the Bible talks about partaking in an unworthy manner it is talking more about mocking and making fun of the sacrifice of Jesus; not respecting what the Lord finished for us. If you partake that way, you are opening up a door in your life for the devil (not God) to come in and cause you all kind of problems; so don't mock the things of God even if you don't understand them. Humble yourself before the Lord and let Him know that you are willing and expecting to receive the manifestation of His goodness and grace in your life.

Now, here is something we have not had a lot of teaching on concerning what the Lord meant about judging ourselves. In those verses, He said that if we take the bread and wine in an unworthy way we can bring judgment on ourselves. How? By not discerning the Lord's body, and He said that was why many were sick and also died. They did not get sick and die because there was a sin in their life they forgot to confess before they ate the bread; as if they had 20 sins in their life, but the Lord knew that they only confessed 19 of them so He struck them dead. God is not trying to scare His people off from taking communion.

Matter of fact, because of God's grace in our lives, Jesus took and bore all of our judgement. God is not judging us. He can chasten us through negative situations and teach us how to avoid pitfalls in life, but He doesn't cause bad things in our lives so He can chasten us or teach us something. He prefers that we learn through His Word; that's the best and easiest way. If I tell my child not to touch the burner on the stove when it's turned on and the child does it anyway; that was not my fault, but I will take the opportunity to teach my child a lesson from it. The

Lord said that if we would judge ourselves we would not be judged. He is not just talking about possible sins we have committed, but He is especially talking about rightly judging and understanding what Jesus did for us through His death and resurrection. In II Corinthians 5:14, the Apostle Paul said, **"For the love of Christ compels us, because <u>we judge thus</u>: that if One died for all, then all died."**

This is the same thing Paul was talking about. He said that we make this judgement. What judgement? In the dictionary, this word means **"The ability to make considered decisions or come to sensible conclusions."** When he said that we make this judgement, he was saying that we consider this decision and come to this conclusion that if Jesus died for everyone then everyone died in Him. He first came to the conclusion that if I died in Christ when He died, then it was my old man (nature of sin and death) that died, and is therefore dead right now. The old man I used to be is dead and removed out of my spirit, and I am a brand new man inside. Every Christian needs to make that judgement!

Another great judgement or decision you can make when you take the Lord's Supper is that since Jesus healed my body by His 39 stripes, then I am healed right now. I believe the main reason Paul said that many were weak, sick and dying is because they did not make that judgement or come to that conclusion concerning healing for their bodies. So, when you partake of communion, remember to judge yourself so you will not be judged. Make the right decisions and come to the right conclusions based on God's Word and our redemption in Christ.

CHAPTER
7

HAVE YOU FOUND YOURSELF?

Did you know that you can find yourself through understanding your Blood covenant with God? You can find out who you really are, and who you really are might surprise you, and it will definitely amaze you! Finding yourself involves much more than just you alone, because your true self, now that you are born again, is not just about you, but it's all about Jesus and your union with Him.

Christians and non-Christians alike will spend time searching the internet and any other avenues where information is available to find out about their family tree. They want to know where they came from and details about their ancestry. They will spend hours and hours of time studying and digging through any glimmer of information that could possibly relate to them. They don't consider it a waste of time at all. They act like it is a great priority that must be accomplished in their lives. I wish that these same Christians would spend as much time and effort studying and meditating the Word of God to discover their true identity as a born-again spirit man in Christ Jesus!

When Christians use that much time studying their family tree; they are really only learning about the history of their physical bodies. When you are obtaining more knowledge about where your past relatives were born and what kind of lives they lived, it's satisfying your curiosity, and yes, it can be interesting and enlightening; but you are not learning about the real you. The real you, is the spirit man or spirit woman in your body that has been made a new creation in Christ. He is the one you want to know about and he's the one you want to dedicate your time and effort to learn about!

So, as a Believer, when I ask you if you have found yourself, I am not asking to see if you know where you were born or if you know all the details of your ancestral tree. Also, I am not enquiring as to whether you are a Christian or not. I want to know if you have found yourself after the new birth experience. In other words, now that you have received and confessed Jesus as your Lord and Savior, have you found yourself? I am talking about discovering who you really are in Christ. How well do you know the new you? A similar question I could ask you is the question the Jewish priests and Levites asked John the Baptist in John 1:22, "<u>What do you say about yourself?</u>" That question would also make a good title for this chapter, wouldn't it?

Did you know that the Lord Jesus found Himself? He knew exactly who He was didn't He? Look with me at Luke 4:16-21.

"So He came to Nazareth, where He had been brought up. And as His custom was, He went into the synagogue on the Sabbath day, and stood up to read.
And He was handed the book of the prophet Isaiah. And when He had opened the book, He found the place where it was written:
"The Spirit of the Lord is upon Me, because He has anointed Me to preach the gospel to the poor; He has sent Me to heal the brokenhearted, to proclaim liberty to the captives and recovery of sight to the blind, to set at liberty those who are oppressed; to proclaim the acceptable year of the Lord."
Then He closed the book, and gave it back to the attendant and sat down. And the eyes of all who were in the synagogue were fixed on Him.
And He began to say to them, "Today this Scripture is fulfilled in your hearing."" (Emphasis added through out chapter)

After Jesus was successful in overcoming the devil's three tests, He came into the synagogue in Nazareth. The Bible says that He stood up to read and was handed the book of Isaiah. Of course, the book of Isaiah is part of our Bible today. He didn't have the New Testament back then but He did have the writings of the prophet Isaiah. When He opened the book, <u>He found the place</u> where it was written, and in this case, it was Isaiah chapter 61. What did He find? What was He looking for? The same thing we need to be looking for today. <u>He was looking for Himself</u>. If the Lord Jesus needed to find Himself, how much more do you and I need to find ourselves! When He began to quote the Scripture, "The Spirit of the Lord is upon <u>Me</u>..." He was actually identifying Himself to the people. wasn't He? He knew those Scriptures were talking about Him.

The Lord identified Himself as the Messiah they had been waiting for, which should have been very good news, but the people did not think so. They totally rejected Him. They got so mad at what He said that they tried to throw Him off a cliff. Everything He said was the truth and good news, but as far as they were concerned it did not matter. They were so spiritually blinded and bound by man's religious ideas that they could not see the real truth. If you think about it, Jesus was an itinerant teacher and preacher and this was the beginning of His travelling ministry. You could say that this was His first seminar to launch His ministry; yet it went very badly, didn't it? You know the pastor of that church did not invite Him back for another meeting. Jesus probably did not pick up any monthly financial partners or sell any ministry materials either.

If the people in that synagogue did not listen to what Jesus had to say, then don't be surprised if you encounter people with that same kind of attitude. Even though you will meet people that prefer darkness instead of light, don't let that discourage you because God will send you to people that want to hear the Gospel and receive all that God has for them. Let's take a lesson here from the Master. Despite an entire church congregation wanting to murder Him, that did not stop Him from continuing on in His travelling ministry. He was totally focused on His purpose for coming to this earth. We need to be just as focused and determined as our Lord was. Don't let anything stop you from serving the Lord with all your heart and fulfilling all that He has called you to do! Always walk and live by faith in God, and always walk in love and forgiveness towards all people!

Don't ever lose sight of why you are here! Don't lose your vision! Keep it ever before you! If you don't know why you are here or what your vision is, then that is a good sign that you need to spend more time finding yourself. If you are wondering how to do that, just follow Jesus' example. How did He find Himself? **In the Word of God**! Like I have already said, if Jesus needed to find Himself then we definitely need to find ourselves! And we are going to have to do it the same way that He did. Get serious about spending time every day in God's Word looking for yourself; not just quickly trying to read through the Bible so that you can say that you read it again. From now on read and meditate the Word with a purpose, a strong inner resolve to find yourself! You're in there! Your name may not be in there, but you are; that is, the real you in Christ is in there!

I guarantee you that if the church you attend took a group picture of the entire congregation and gave you a copy of it, the first thing you would do is to find yourself in that photo. As soon as you find yourself in the picture, you would then tell everyone around you where you are located so they can see your face. You would be excited about that wouldn't you? Well, you should be even more excited about finding yourself in the Bible.   Let me remind you of one of the best ways to find yourself in the Bible. Look for the verses that describe who you are in Christ, in Him and in the Lord. Please see our book "IN CHRIST…" for more detailed teaching on that.

If you are reading in Romans 8:1 and it says that there is no condemnation to those in Christ, you just found yourself. You might want to stop right there and say, "I found myself! I am in Christ; therefore, the Lord is talking about me! Wow! That is really me!   I don't have any condemnation because I am in Christ. That is a description of my true (spiritual) self! That is who I am right now!" When you start finding out who you really are, then quit talking about who you used to be! Quit talking about the person who is no longer you! That person is dead and gone; so let him stay dead! Quit trying to resurrect him! Remember, your old self (the nature of sin and death) was crucified with Christ! He died with Christ and was buried with Him also! He (your old spiritual nature) is dead and removed out of your spirit! When Jesus was made alive, so were you! You were made alive into a new man (person) in Him! God resurrected you together with Christ Jesus and seated you at His right hand in the Heavenly places in Christ!

Do you understand what I am talking about? You have to start by finding yourself in Christ at Calvary. If you are not sure what Scriptures you should study concerning this, then please get our book "The Mystery" and "The Mystery Study Guide" for further help. Another area where we need to find ourselves is in the area of healing. Maybe you haven't thought about it like that before. When you spend time studying the healing Scriptures you are finding out some things about yourself concerning what Jesus did for your physical body. Have you found yourself in Christ concerning financial prosperity? Have you found yourself in Christ about having a successful marriage? Have you found yourself in Christ in how to win the lost to Jesus and fulfill God's calling on your life? Can you see that finding yourself in Him involves every area of your life?

Let's go back to that Scripture about John the Baptist and look at something else over there.

"Then they said to him, "Who are you, that we may give an answer to those who sent us? What do you say about yourself?"
He said, "I am the voice of one crying in the wilderness: make straight the way of the Lord" as the prophet Isaiah said.""

When they asked him, "What do you say about yourself" they were asking him if he found himself weren't they? His answer was a definite "Yes" wasn't it? How did he find himself? In the Scriptures, obviously he took time to study the book of Isaiah until he found himself. He quoted a verse out of the book of Isaiah. Can you quote Scriptures out of the Bible, especially the epistles (the letters written to the Church) that describe who you are? If you can't, then you need to make that a major priority in your life!! You must know that you know what your true identity is in Christ or the devil will run all over you!

I want you to go back with me for just a minute to the book of Genesis. There was a man named Adam, and this man originally knew who he was. He knew his identity as a son of God. didn't he? But something happened to him. Instead of Adam finding himself, he actually lost himself when he disobeyed the Lord. When he ate of the fruit of the tree he died spiritually and was separated from God.

He lost the life of God in his spirit and received spiritual death in its place. Here is what the Lord asked Adam in Genesis 3:9, **"Then the Lord God called to Adam and said to him, "Where are you?"**

God did not ask Adam this question because he did not know his geographical location. God is all knowing and He knew exactly where Adam was. What was the Lord saying to Adam through that question? He was saying that Adam lost himself. Instead of finding himself, he lost himself. He did not lose himself geographically, but spiritually. So, what did he lose? His life was separated from the source of all life. He lost his spiritual position as a son of Almighty God. He lost the headship, authority and blessing the Lord placed upon him. He also lost his faith or ability to receive from God. Now, by understanding what Adam lost, you can see what a person gains when he finds himself in Christ.

Let me remind you of another story; it's about the lame man who was healed at the Gate Beautiful in Acts 3:3-6.

"Who, seeing Peter and John about to go into the temple, asked for alms.
And fixing his eyes on him, with John, Peter said, "Look at us."
So he gave them his attention, expecting to receive something from them.

Then Peter said, "Silver and gold I do not have, but what I do have I give you: In the name of Jesus Christ of Nazareth, rise up and walk."" (Emphasis added throughout chapter)

The Apostle Peter said, "Look at us." Why did he say that? Did he say that because he was full of pride and thought that he was better than the lame man? Of course not! Did he say that because he considered himself the healer and not Jesus? Of course not! Well, then why did he say, "Look at us?" He said it that way because he knew who he was in Christ. He knew that he had something for the man. He knew that He and the Healer were one. He knew that he was in a Blood covenant with God, the One who created our physical bodies, and he knew that God could heal people through him!

Peter wasn't being arrogant at all; he had great confidence in the greater One within him! He did not see himself as being alone or by himself. I am not saying that he knew he wasn't alone because John was there. Spiritually, he knew that he was not alone. He knew that he was in Christ and Christ was in him! When he said to look at us, he was saying, "I want you to see Jesus the healer in me. He wants to express Himself through me by healing your body." As you know, the lame man was instantly healed and made whole, then in verse 12 of that same chapter, Peter clarifies that he did not heal the man, but Jesus did.

"So when Peter saw it, he responded to the people: "Men of Israel, why do you marvel at this? Or why look so intently at us, as though by our own power or godliness we had made this man walk?""

Peter told the people that this healing miracle for the lame man was not done by him personally. He did not have any healing power apart from Christ; yet Peter knew that he was not apart from Christ. He knew that he was an earthen vessel that God could manifest the excellence of His power through (II Corinthians 4:7). Do you know that about your life? Are you totally convinced of your union with Christ Jesus; that He is in you and you are in Him? If you are, then you know that God can do anything in your life and through you for others, if you will just yield to the Holy Spirit and allow Him to have His way in you. Here is example from the Apostle Paul's life.

"And as they bound him with thongs, Paul said to the centurion who stood by, "Is it lawful for you to scourge a man who is a Roman, and uncondemned?"
When the centurion heard that, he went and told the commander, saying, "Take care what you do, for this man is a Roman."
Then the commander came and said to him, "Tell me, are you a Roman?" He said, "Yes."
The commander answered, "With a large sum I obtained this citizenship." And Paul said, "But I was born a citizen."

Then immediately those who were about to examine him withdrew from him; and the commander was also afraid after he found out that he was a Roman, and because he had bound him."

I like this story because it is a good example of the importance of knowing who you are, not just in the spirit realm but also in the natural realm. Just don't spend all your time studying who you are naturally to the neglect of who you are spiritually. If you noticed in those verses, the commander told Paul that he paid a large sum to obtain his citizenship, didn't he? I guess he thought that would impress Paul, but Paul responded by telling the commander that he was born a citizen. I like that. Paul said, "I was born this way." Listen! If you are born again, then you have been born a new man in Christ! Spiritually, you can say, "I was born that way! I am born of the Spirit of God! I have been born into the Kingdom and family of God! Right now, I am a son of God! Right now, I am God's righteousness in Christ!"

Why did Paul tell the commander that he was born a Roman citizen? Because he knew that as a Roman citizen he had rights that non-Romans did not have. He knew that he had benefits he could appropriate. Naturally speaking, Paul expected to enjoy and experience every right that was his as a Roman citizen! How much more we as citizens of the Kingdom of God should expect to enjoy and experience all of our Divine rights as sons of God in Christ Jesus! The problem is, if you haven't found yourself in Christ then you will not be aware of your Christian rights. The Apostle Paul was highly developed in his identity in Christ and in the fact that he was in a Blood covenant with God. Do you remember his testimony before he found himself in Christ?

"I persecuted this Way to the death, binding and delivering into prisons both men and women,

As also the high priest bears me witness, and all the council of the elders, from whom I also received letters to the brethren, and went to Damascus to bring in chains even those who were there to Jerusalem to be punished." (Acts 22:4-5)

When Paul was lost and was called Saul, he was like a hitman for the devil and his kingdom wasn't he? After he was born again and became Paul, he began to find himself. God gave him a revelation that Saul (the old man) was dead, and he was a brand new man in Christ. He had such a reality of what it meant to be a brand new man, that he could say, **"Therefore I testify to you this day that I am innocent of the blood of all men."** (Acts 20:26). Obviously, Paul believed, without a doubt, that his old man (the nature of sin and death) was dead and gone; really gone!

The Paul he was in Christ was not the Paul (or person) who persecuted Christians to the death and delivered them into prisons. That was a completely different man! Are we developed today that strongly in our identity in Christ? We need to be!! Let's get that developed!! We need to follow Paul's example! When you can say the same thing about yourself as he did then you have truly found yourself in Christ Jesus. I know that your past may not be identical to Paul's, but you still had a past, an old man, and you need to believe, without a doubt, that he is dead and gone! Listen to what Paul said in Philippians 3:7-10.

"But what things were gain to me, these I have counted loss for Christ.

Yet indeed I also count all things loss for the excellence of the knowledge of Christ Jesus my Lord, for whom I have suffered the loss of all things, and count them as rubbish, that I may gain Christ.

And <u>be found in Him</u>, not having my own righteousness, which is from the law, but that which is through faith in Christ, the righteousness which is from God by faith;

<u>That I may know Him</u> and the power of His resurrection, and the fellowship of His sufferings, being conformed to His death."

It seems that the most important thing to Paul was to find himself in Christ and to know Him. So, after a person comes to know Jesus as their Lord and Savior, that's not the end of their quest, and it's not the end of their adventure, but it is the very beginning. Can you hear the cry and the earnest desire of Paul's heart in those verses? He wanted to be found in Christ and to know Him. That is what I want, how about you? You may be thinking, "Well, I already know the Lord." I don't doubt that you know Him more than you did before you got saved, but you can know Him much, much more. I knew a lot about my wife after we had been married for one month, but after eight years, I know her a whole lot better. Paul also said,

"Not that I have already attained, or am already perfected; but I press on, that I may lay hold of that for which Christ Jesus has also laid hold of me.

Brethren, I do not count myself to have apprehended; but one thing I do, forgetting those things which are behind and reaching forward to those things which are ahead.

I press toward the goal for the prize of the upward call of God in Christ Jesus." (Philippians 3:12-14)

When he said that he was not perfected, he was talking about in his soul and body. If you don't realize this you need to. You are already perfect in your spirit in Christ (Ephesians 4:24; Hebrews 10:14). Now, our life on this earth is about yielding to the Holy Spirit and allowing Him to continually take everything that God has deposited in our spirits and manifest them in our souls and bodies. This is what Paul was talking about when he said, **"...I press on, that I may lay hold of that for which Christ Jesus has**

also laid hold of me." The King James Bible says, **"…That I may apprehend that for which also I am apprehended of Christ Jesus."** God's Word Translation says, **"…But I run to win that which Jesus Christ has already won for me."**

Were you listening to those verses? The Lord Jesus has already laid hold of, apprehended and won everything for you and me! He has already paid our penalty for sin, healed us, delivered us, made us prosperous and very wise! He has already finished everything for us and given us every good thing that Heaven has to offer! All of these things are already done for us, but they will not automatically appear in our lives just because they are finished. Knowing that Jesus has already apprehended all good things for us is called <u>grace</u>. Knowing that we must lay hold of and apprehend all that He finished for us is called <u>faith</u>. When you learn how to operate in grace and faith, you will experience God's supernatural rest. In closing this chapter, I want to mention that if you would like more teaching on this subject. I have 25 audio messages (about 13 minutes each) on Youtube; just go on youtube.com and type in "Dwayne Norman Have you found yourself".

CHAPTER
8

PLEADING THE BLOOD
OF JESUS

There is such great and awesome power in the precious Blood of Jesus! I am so glad to be under grace in this new Blood covenant with God! It's a new and better covenant established upon better promises, isn't it? This dispensation of grace in which we live today is greater than we can imagine, but before our Lord shed His Blood for us, God's people operated under the dispensation of law. The Lord had to work through the blood of animals to provide atonement for man's sins. Let me remind you of the Exodus story, the deliverance of God's people; specifically, when they put the blood on their homes to protect their firstborn from death. This is what the Lord spoke to Moses and Aaron in Exodus 12:3-7,

"Speak to all the congregation of Israel, saying: 'On the tenth of this month <u>every man shall take for himself a lamb</u>, according to the house of his father, <u>a lamb for a household</u>.

'And if the household is too small for the lamb, let him and his neighbor next to his house take it according to the number of the persons; according to each man's need you shall make your count for the lamb.

'<u>Your lamb shall be without blemish</u>, a male of the first year. You may take it from the sheep or from the goats.

'Now you shall keep it until the fourteenth day of the same month. Then the whole assembly of the congregation of Israel shall kill it at twilight.

'And <u>they shall take some of the blood</u> and put it on the two doorposts and on the lintel of the houses where they eat it."   (Emphasis added throughout chapter)

The Lord said that every man had to take a lamb for their household and <u>they</u> (not God) had to apply or put the blood on their houses. Or you could say they had to apply the blood to their lives. Even though we don't use the blood of animals anymore, we still have Blood to apply to our lives today, and it is the all-powerful Blood of Jesus. Many Christians have called it "Pleading the Blood". There are not any verses in the Bible that use that exact phrase, but what it means is very Scriptural and very important for us to understand. But, before we talk about pleading the Blood, I want to look at something else in Exodus 12: 8-13.

"Then they shall eat the flesh on that night; roasted in fire, with unleavened bread and with bitter herbs they shall eat it.

Do not eat it raw, nor boiled at all with water, but roasted in fire-its head with its legs and its entrails.

You shall let none of it remain until morning, and what remains of it until morning you shall burn with fire.

And thus you shall eat it: with a belt on your waist, your sandals on your feet, and your staff in your hand. So you shall eat it in haste. It is the Lord's Passover.

For I will pass through the land of Egypt on that night, and will strike all the firstborn in the land of Egypt, both man and beast; and against all the gods of Egypt I will execute judgment: I am the Lord.

Now the blood shall be a sign for you on the houses where you are. And <u>when I see the blood, I will pass over you</u>; and the plague shall not be on you to destroy you when I strike the land of Egypt.

Sometimes when you hear how God instructed them to eat all of the lamb or sacrifice, it doesn't sound to appetizing does it? What we need to understand is why He told them this. Laying their hands on the lamb and eating of it was all about identification with the sacrifice. They were in a blood covenant with God, and the lamb they offered was a type of Christ, the Lamb of God who shed His Blood through death. For us today, being in this **new** Blood covenant with God is all about relationship, oneness with the Lord and total identification with Him in His entire substitutionary sacrifice. Now think about this with me. Jesus of course was our representative in this new covenant, but He was also our sacrifice as well. He was both wasn't He? He was our Blood sacrifice to validate and authenticate the covenant, and He was our representative before God the Father so we could enter into the covenant.

In the verses we just read, the Bible said that the Lamb had to be without blemish, didn't it? The lamb or sacrifice had to be spotless, but not the person offering the sacrifice. The person offering the lamb did not have to be sinless or spotless; only the sacrifice did. It is very important that you understand this. Sometimes when witnessing to a lost person, he will say to me, "I will receive Jesus as soon as I quit drinking, smoking, lying and cheating, or as soon as I get my life cleaned up." Whether he understands it or not, he is acting like he is the sacrifice needed for his redemption and not Jesus. He thinks his salvation is based on his performance, on what he can do to clean up his life so that God will accept him. He does not have a reality of the importance of Jesus' sacrifice.

Ephesians 1:6 says that God has made us accepted in the Beloved. If you are in Christ, you are already accepted with God. There is nothing you can do through your good works to become any more accepted! So, this lost person does not understand that his life is not the sacrifice offered to redeem mankind. He doesn't understand that his salvation is not based upon what sins he has committed or has not committed. His salvation is based solely on the Lord Jesus Christ. He was our sacrifice, and He was sinless and perfect, so we did not have to be. I like to tell lost people that if they will receive Jesus into their lives then He will give them the power to clean up their lives. He will give them His holiness and righteousness to walk in. He will give them the strength and ability to be all that God wants them to be.

Almost 2,000 years ago, the sinless Lamb of God took away all of our sin (the sin nature) and all the sins we had committed and will ever commit. We did not do it; He did it! He paid our penalty for sin and finished everything for us at Calvary! In our reborn spirits we are now perfect, holy and righteous in Christ Jesus (Ephesians 4:24)! It's our minds and bodies that have to be trained and developed to put on the new man, to put on Christ. When we put on the Lord Jesus Christ, we will not make any provision for the flesh, to fulfill its lusts (Galatians 3:27; Romans 13:14).

As I have said before, it is time for Christians to learn how to live from the inside out. It is time to learn how to live out of the fullness of the Godhead in Christ in our spirits! Then we will rule and reign as kings in life and subdue and take dominion over everything the devil brings against us! Our faith in Jesus is our victory that has overcome this world! Right now, we are sons of God because of the Blood of Jesus shed for us through His entire sacrifice. Our Heavenly Father only sees us in Christ and through His Blood, and that is how we should see ourselves. Since God sees us that way, it's ok for you and me to see ourselves that way. When we see ourselves the way God does, then we will have no fear and we will be strong in faith!

Now, let's go back to Exodus chapter 12, we read where God said that when He saw the blood He would pass over them and the destroyer would not harm them. Let me ask you a few questions here. When was God talking about seeing the blood? Was it when they killed the lamb? Didn't He see the lamb shed its blood when they killed it? Of course, He did, but that was not what He was talking about. Remember, He told them to put some of the blood on the doorposts and on the lintel of their houses. In other words, the Lord did not see the blood as protection for them until they applied it. Even though the blood had been shed by the lamb, if they had not applied it (or as we would say today, "If they did not plead the blood"), the destroyer would have killed them.

Think about that with me. Today, Jesus our supreme sacrifice has shed His blood for you and me, and obtained healing, deliverance, protection and prosperity, but until you and I apply or plead the Blood we can miss out on all those wonderful blessings. For Christians today, the question should not be, "Did God the Father see Jesus shed His Blood?" The questions should be, "Did you through God's Word see Jesus shed His Blood? Do you understand what the Lord accomplished for you when He shed His Blood, died and arose from the dead? Do you know how to apply His precious Blood to your life today?"

When I talk about pleading the Blood of Jesus, I am talking about using our faith to appropriate and experience all that our Lord finished for us at Calvary by His grace. When you plead the Blood in faith against the devil or over a person or situation, you are saying, "I believe in all that Jesus did for me through His entire Blood sacrifice, and that's what I expect to be manifested and demonstrated in this situation, in my family, marriage, job, finances and town!"

When you plead the Blood, you are acknowledging all that Jesus' Blood stands for, and that includes your entire redemption. When you plead the Blood of Jesus against the devil, you are hitting him with the full force of Calvary! You are reminding him of how Jesus defeated him and crushed his head under His feat! You are also reminding devil that everything Jesus did to him, you did to him, because you are in Christ! I Peter 5:8-9 say:

"Be sober, be vigilant; because your adversary the devil walks about like a roaring lion, seeking whom he may devour.
Resist him, steadfast in the faith, knowing that the same sufferings are experienced by your brotherhood in the world."

The word "Adversary" in the Greek language means an opponent in a lawsuit. A lot of times, resisting the devil is a lot like a court case and not a battle field. The devil is our adversary; he is the one bringing the lawsuit against us. Your attorney is Jesus (I John 2:1). When the judge motions to your attorney (Jesus) to begin, He then calls for the perfect witness on your behalf; His own Blood! Jesus' Blood cries out to the Judge of the universe (our Father God), you are innocent; the man (old man) who committed those crimes is dead! You are a new man in Christ, all your sins have been washed away, and you are healed, free and abundantly blessed! You have all authority and dominion in Jesus' Name over the devil and all of hell! That is what the devil hears when you plead the Blood of Jesus over your life and over any situation! Isaiah 43:26, in the King James Bible says:

"Put me in remembrance: let us plead together: declare thou, that thou mayest be justified."

In the Dictionary, the word "Plead" means to present and argue for (a position), especially in court or in another public context. The Lord did not ask us to put Him in remembrance because He forgot what he said. He will never forget what He did for us, how He redeemed us back to Himself through His Son's sacrifice. Like we talked about in the chapter on Communion, remembering what Jesus did for us means more than telling us not to forget that Jesus died for us, but it was to remind us again and again that we can experience all that He finished for us right now in our lives.

When we plead the Blood, we are not only remembering all that Jesus' Blood did for us, but just like in a court case, we are acknowledging that it was legally done for us and there is nothing the devil (the prosecutor) can do to legally override that. The Lord Jesus presented His sinless Blood to our Father (the Judge) in His throne room as evidence of our eternal redemption. Our enemy (the devil) does not have a legal right to put sickness, poverty, fear, depression or any of the curse on us! You have a legal right to resist what he brings against you and to expect it to leave in Jesus' Name!

Forever the Blood of Jesus speaks and testifies on your behalf that you have been acquitted, found not guilty, and that you have all authority and dominion over the one who keeps trying to prosecute you! According to James 4:7, if you will submit to God, which is submitting to the authority of His Word, and resist the devil, he will flee from you! Expect your enemy to run in stark terror from you every time you resist and rebuke him in the Name of Jesus! Expect it!! **This is a legal matter that has been settled forever in the court of Heaven! Praise God!**

The words "I plead the Blood of Jesus" are not some kind of Christian magical words we say. It's very important that you believe and understand the Blood covenant you are in with God, and what Jesus did for you through His Blood. I can tell you right now that the devil knows what the Blood of Jesus means, he also knows how powerful it is, and he does not want you to find out. He wants to keep you in the dark when it comes to your Blood covenant rights in Christ. Whenever you plead the Blood of Jesus, always do it in faith. In case you are not sure how to release your faith, I want to remind you of a couple of Scriptures.

"So Jesus answered and said to them, "Have faith in God.
For assuredly, I say to you, whoever says to this mountain, 'Be removed and be cast into the sea,' and does not doubt in his heart, but believes that those things he says will be done, he will have whatever he says."" (Mark 11:22-23)

"(As it is written, I have made thee a father of many nations") before him whom he believed, even God, who quickeneth the dead, and calleth those things which be not as though they were." (Romans 4:17, King James Bible)

Whether you realize it or not, the Lord Jesus originated the phrase "You can have what you say"; so if you are one of those Christians who mock people of faith with comments like "That name it and claim it bunch or blab it and grab it group" you are actually making fun of and mocking what your Lord and Savior said, and you are mocking your own salvation. Jesus did not say that we can have just anything we say, without placing a big contingency on that statement. He said that if we do not doubt in our hearts, but believe in our hearts, truly believe, that what we say will come to pass, then we will have what we say. If you think you are using your faith in God to believe Him for $1,000,000 and you have never used your faith for $100, you probably will not get the $1,000,000. Just saying that you have a million dollars is not good enough. You must believe in your heart that what you say will come to pass or it will not.

The Apostle Paul said that our faith grows (II Thessalonians 1:3). It is just like lifting weights, we have to start with the amount of weight that we can bench press now and continue to add more to it as time goes on. Start practicing using your faith and it will develop and grow. The only way you will have what you say is when you get your mouth in agreement with what you believe in your heart.

So, here is what I mean about releasing my faith when I plead or speak the Blood of Jesus. Whenever I say, "Father, I plead Jesus' Blood as a protective covering over my wife, my children, me and all that we have in Jesus' Name", I believe in my heart that what I say will come to pass. Just having a positive confession is not enough. Just having positive thoughts is not enough either. It is not about my mouth and head coming into agreement. It is about my mouth and heart coming into agreement. I must believe in my heart that what I say will be manifested! Therefore, I believe in my heart that God's Divine protection by His power and angels belong to me and my family because of what Jesus did for me through His Blood shed at Calvary. I believe in my heart that the devil and his curse cannot touch us; they have to go on down the road because we are covered in and soaked in the precious Blood of Jesus!

According to the Scripture you just read in Romans 4:17, we, as Believers, need to spend more time calling those things which be not as though they were; that is the same as confessing and declaring out of our mouths what we believe in your hearts will come to pass. Our Heavenly Father set the example for us when He created the worlds in the beginning.

What did He do when He wanted light to come forth where there was darkness? He called those things which be not (or be not manifested in the natural realm) as though they were (or were manifested). He believed what He said would come to pass before it had come to pass. That is called operating in faith or releasing your faith.

Hebrews 11:3 tells us that God used His faith to frame the worlds. So, if you want to say it a different way, you could say that God named it and claimed it. He said, "Light be" and light was. He called light into existence, didn't He? In Ephesians 5:1, the Lord tells you and me to imitate Him, and in other Scriptures He tells us to walk and live by faith. Everything we say and do should be by our faith in God, therefore when we plead the Blood of Jesus, we always release faith and expect to see results!

I remember one time when my brother and I were out witnessing and a man pulled a homemade 22 pistol on us. He stuck the gun in my car asking me for a ride. While the gun was almost touching the temple of my head, I spoke this out loud, not to the man but to the devil. I said Satan, "I bind you in Jesus' Name and I break your power over this man doing this to me, and I command you to stop right now!" I soon as I said that, the man pulled his gun out of my car, threw it onto the side walk and walk off into the dark and never came back. God protected us and delivered us out of that situation because of the power in the Blood of Jesus!!

There was another night when I was talking to a man about receiving the Lord and he said to me, "What will you do if I pull my knife out and threaten to cut you up in little pieces?" I just looked him straight in the eyes and said, "I am not going to do anything. I am just going to stand here and watch what happens to you." I stood there and kept looking him right in the eyes until he became nervous. He started looking over his left and right shoulders wondering if I had someone else with me. He then looked back at me and said, "You are just a kook anyway," and he turned and left, but the Lord protected me again from the devil's plans. For almost 3 years, God protected me and my brother while witnessing to prostitutes and pimps in Dallas, Texas. There is Divine protection in the Blood of Jesus!

Another time I was coming home from a meeting during a cold winter. I was crossing over the West Virginia Mountains, going about 35 miles an hour on the interstate. The roads were totally covered with snow and ice. I was driving very close to the edge of a cliff when all of a sudden, I lost control of the car and it was about to head off the cliff. Loudly, I said, "Jesus!" I didn't have time to say anything else. Immediately, I felt someone grab the back of my car and put it back on the road! I believe it was an angel of God. The Lord saved my life that night! I believe in the all-powerful covenant Blood of Jesus! I believe in pleading and speaking the Blood over everything! When I plead the Blood, I am declaring that I have all authority and dominion over the devil, sickness, poverty, death and evil of every kind!!

I plead the Blood of Jesus (not legalistically but in faith) over me and my family every day! I believe in the Divine protection that it ours through Jesus' precious Blood! Every blessing and benefit in Jesus' Blood belongs to you and me because we are in union with Him through this new and eternal Blood covenant! Take advantage of your covenant rights! Walk in the fullness of who you are in Christ! Don't take anything off of the devil! Crush his head under your feet everywhere you go and have fun preaching the Gospel and winning the lost to Jesus every day! Revelation 12:11 says,

"And they overcame him by the blood of the Lamb and by the word of their testimony, and they did not love their lives to the death."

This verse is talking about God's people overcoming the accuser of the brethren (the devil). How did they do it? Did they overcome the devil just because he knew they were redeemed by Jesus' Blood? No, the devil's knowledge of what Jesus did at Calvary is not what enabled the Believers to overcome him. What I am getting at is that they (the

Believers) had to say or confess something. They did not experience their victory because of the devil's knowledge of Calvary. It was because of their knowledge and what they believed and declared belonged to them through the shed Blood of Jesus. They had to release their faith in the grace of God. They overcame by the Blood of the Lamb and the word of their testimony. It sounds to me like, in some fashion, they were pleading the Blood. They were acknowledging what Jesus did for them through His sacrifice and how He saved them.

In the old covenant God said that the life of the flesh is in the blood.

"For the life of the flesh is in the blood, and I have given it to you upon the altar to make atonement for your souls; for it is the blood that makes atonement for the soul." (Leviticus 17:11)

The blood of animals was used to make atonement for or to be a covering for man, to cleanse him outwardly but not inwardly. Animal blood could not actually cleanse man's conscience and make him righteous, but the Blood of Jesus could. Hebrews 9:12-14 says:

"Not with the blood of goats and calves, but with His own blood He entered the Most Holy Place once for all, having obtained eternal redemption.

For if the blood of bulls and goats and the ashes of a heifer, sprinkling the unclean, sanctifies for the purifying of the flesh,

How much more shall the blood of Christ, who through the eternal Spirit offered Himself without spot to God, cleanse your conscience from dead works to serve the living God?"

Hebrews 7:16 says: "Who (Jesus) has come, not according to the law of a fleshly commandment, but according to the power of an endless life."

This endless life that our Lord has is in His Blood. It is resurrection life! Since the life of the flesh is in the blood, then the resurrection life of Jesus is in His Blood, and because His Blood is covenant Blood, that brings you and me into the picture. There is an eternal connection between you and His resurrection life. We are filled with His endless, resurrection life because we are one with Jesus; totally united together in Blood covenant with Him.

"Therefore, brethren, having boldness to enter the Holiest by the blood of Jesus." (Hebrews 10:19)

Our Heavenly Father imposed on us and made a new Blood covenant with us; thereby redeeming us and washing us white as snow in Jesus' Blood. His holy Blood which was poured out for you and me is now available for us to apply and speak forth (plead) in faith to receive into our lives all the finished works of Christ! Let's be bold to plead the Blood of Jesus! God has given us boldness! We have full access into God's presence and throne room through Jesus' Blood (Ephesians 3:12). We not only have full access but we are permanently seated there in Christ! We carry the presence of the Lord everywhere we go because we are the temple of the Holy Spirit on this earth! Everything in the precious Blood of Jesus belongs to you and me today through our covenant with the Lord.

When you plead the Blood, you are speaking forth and releasing all the resurrection life and power of God into a person's life or into any given situation! So believe it and expect it to be so! Jesus shed His Blood in the Garden of Gethsemane, He shed His Blood by the 39 stripes He bore for our healing, He shed His Blood by the crown of thorns on His head, by the nails through His hands and feet and by the spear that was thrust into His side. When you truly believe in and plead the Blood of Jesus, the Word of God and your testimony become a sharp sword in your mouth that will cut through all darkness in a person's life and destroy every chain and yoke of bondage! Expect the resurrection life of Jesus to go into them and resurrect everything the devil tried to kill!

Also, there is something else I want you to see. The anointing of the Holy Spirit always works with and through the Blood of Jesus in this new covenant, but before we look at that, let me remind you of how God's anointing and the blood of animals worked together in the old covenant. Back then they were just types and shadows of the reality of what we have now in Christ by God's grace. Leviticus 8:6 says, **"Then Moses brought Aaron and his sons and washed them with water."** In the Bible, water is symbolic for the Holy Spirit and for the Word of God. Ephesians 5:26 says, **"That He might sanctify and cleanse her** (the Church) **with the washing of water by the word."** Water cleanses things.

The Blood of Jesus also cleanses. We have been born again by the incorruptible Word of God (I Peter 1:23). We have been cleansed by the water of God's Word and washed white as snow by the redeeming Blood of Jesus. When Aaron and his sons were washed with the water, they were not born again and made God's righteousness in Christ like you and me. What they did was a type and shadow of the true substance or reality of our salvation today. Let's continue on in Leviticus 8:12.

"And he poured some of the anointing oil on Aaron's head and anointed him, to consecrate him."

The anointing oil represents the Holy Spirit (the Glory of God) and His power. So, Moses washed them in water and anointed them with oil (or the Holy Spirit). Then listen to what he did after the sacrifice was killed.

"And Moses killed it. Also he took some of its blood and put it on the tip of Aaron's right ear, on the thumb of his right hand, and on the big toe of his right foot.

Then he brought Aaron's sons. And Moses put some of the blood on the tips of their right ears, on the thumbs of their right hands, and on the big toes of their right feet. And Moses sprinkled the blood all around on the altar. (Leviticus 8:23-24)

Putting the blood on the priest's ear, thumb and toe was to show their total consecration, their entire being spirit, soul and body dedicated to the Lord's service. Here is what Dake's Annotated Reference Bible says about these three parts,

"They represent the hearing, working, and walking members of the body. Priests were to hear and obey God and the law, work with their hands in performing their service, and walk in all the ways of God."

As Christians, we are kings and priests in Christ, sanctified and set apart to serve the Lord, all because we have been cleansed by His precious Blood. In your heart and mind, you need to picture and see your total being clothed and saturated in the Blood. It is through the Blood of Jesus that I can hear His voice and obey His Word! It is through the Blood of Jesus that I can lay hands on the sick and see them healed and delivered! It's through His Blood that I have the power and ability to serve Him and walk in all His ways! All that I am and all that I have is soaked in and fully covered in the Blood of the Lamb! When the devil looks at us all he sees is Jesus, and the only color he sees is red! Wow! That is awesome!! Thank you, Lord Jesus for your precious Blood!

"And from Jesus Christ, the faithful witness, the firstborn from the dead, and the ruler over the kings of the earth. To Him who loved us and washed us from our sins in His own blood,
and has made us kings and priests to God and Father, to Him be glory and dominion forever and ever. Amen." (Revelation 1:5-6)

I want us to look at one more verse in Leviticus 8:30 that sums up the priests' consecration through the blood and the anointing oil.

"Then Moses took some of the anointing oil and some of the blood which was on the altar, and sprinkled it on Aaron, on his garments, on his sons, and on the garments of his sons with him; and he consecrated Aaron, his garments, his sons, and the garments of his sons with him."

It sounds like the blood and the anointing oil work together, doesn't it? In the new covenant we need the Blood and the Holy Spirit (the Anointing). They always work together. Remember, it was after Jesus shed His Blood that the Holy Spirit was poured out on the Day of Pentecost. It was after the Lord took His Blood into the Holy of Holies in Heaven that the Spirit of God was able to come into men and women on this earth and recreate their spirits a new and translate them into the Kingdom of God. The Holy Spirit is able to do so much more for us in this new Blood covenant, through Jesus' perfect and sinless Blood, than He could do through the blood of animals. We could not have received the Holy Spirit through the new birth or the baptism in the Spirit without Jesus' redeeming Blood. I John 5:8 says,

"And there are three that bear witness on earth: the Spirit, the water, and the blood; and these three agree as one."

On this earth, the Holy Spirit and the water (I believe the Lord is talking about the water of the Word) agree. So, the Word of God and the Spirit of God agree. The Word of God as you know was given by inspiration of the Holy Spirit, and the Spirit always confirms the Word believed and acted upon. Now, water baptism could be included also because it is an outward demonstration of the inward work of the Spirit of grace in a person's heart.

Always remember that the Holy Spirit, the Word of God and the Blood of Jesus agree. The Holy Spirit is always there to confirm by demonstration all that Jesus did for us through His Blood. He bears witness in our reborn spirits that we are sons of God through the Blood. His supernatural ministry in our lives today is to bring to pass what we prophesy and declare through faith in the Blood. <u>Whenever you honor the Blood of Jesus, the Holy Spirit will always be there to manifest His presence, power and glory</u>.

Romans 3:23 says, **"For all have sinned and fall short of the glory of God."** Before Jesus shed His Blood, mankind had fallen short of the glory of God, but we are not short anymore. I believe that Adam and Eve were originally clothed in God's glory, but what happened when they sinned? The glory left or you could say that they fell short of God's glory. It took the sinless Blood of Jesus to restore the glory of God to man again. As Christians who are washed in the Blood, we are once again clothed in God's glory. It wasn't because of our good works, but it was because of Jesus' good works. Because of the Blood of Jesus in our lives, we are forever clothed and radiant with the glory of God!

Let's expect the glory of God and the power of God to be manifested through us everywhere we go! All the blessings of Heaven are ours in Christ Jesus as partners with God in this awesome Blood covenant! If you don't know what belongs to you then search the Scriptures and find out! Don't miss out on what it means to be filled with all the fullness of God! Don't miss out on the adventure of living by faith! Walk and live every day in all of your Blood covenants rights!

About the Author

Dwayne Norman is a 1978 graduate of Christ For the Nations Bible Institute in Dallas, Texas. He spent 3 years witnessing to prostitutes and pimps in the red-light district of Dallas, and another 3 years ministering as a team leader in the Campus Challenge ministry of Dr. Norvel Hayes. He was ordained by Pastor Buddy and Pat Harrison of Faith Christian Fellowship in Tulsa, Oklahoma in September 1980. He also goes in and teaches at Dr. Hayes' Bible school in Tennessee.

In 1982 the Lord led him to start ministering in churches all over the country. He ministers powerfully on soul winning, and on how God wants to use all Believers in demonstrating His Kingdom not just in Word but also in Power!

He teaches with clarity, the work that God accomplished for all believers in Christ from the cross to the throne, and the importance of this revelation to the church for the fulfillment of Jesus' commission to make disciples of all nations.

He strongly believes that we are called to do the works Jesus did and greater works in His Name, not just in church but especially in the marketplace.

He and his wife Leia travel and teach Supernatural Evangelism, Faith, Grace, Healing and train Believers in who they are in Christ and how to operate in their ministries. He teaches the Word on internet radio Monday through Friday at 4PM Eastern Standard time on wofr.org (The Word of Faith Radio Network). His program is called Victory in the Word. If you would like to hear the radio program on your phone, you can do so by dialing (605) 477-5254 Monday through Friday at 4PM.

He has over 230 audio messages on youtube.com that you can listen to, and he has written 19 teaching books which are available on their ministry website: www.dwaynenormanministries.org Many of his books are also available on amazon.com as Kindle books.

Made in the USA
Columbia, SC
30 October 2017